Meetings with Remarkable Friends
Notes from a Fourth Way School

Rolando Altamirano

BLUE LOGIC

2011

A Blue Logic Publication
P.O. Box 772
Oregon House, CA 95962
www.bluelogic.us

ISBN 978-0-9835253-0-1

Printed in the United States of America

This System works, if you use it.
Robert Burton

CONTENTS

INTRODUCTION

This book comprises a series of essays developed from ideas produced during the different events and articles that appeared in the various publications of the Fellowship of Friends, a living Fourth Way School of our times. These are Work tools and techniques born from necessity; that is, as a response either to an inner question or to a question posed by other students in our School. In some of the essays the original question is mentioned or hinted at, yet in others only an approach to the Work ideas is presented.

The essays are offered in the order they were produced; and there is no real beginning or end to this document. It can be read in any order desired, as one reads a reference book. You may wish to know that the subject is one: the creation and development of what in the System is called the "steward".

This document also shows the way the School was working at the time these ideas were expressed. A School of the Fourth Way is a living organism; and as such it is constantly growing, developing and changing. Most of all, it moves at an increasing speed.

It constantly changes its tools and techniques and introduces new ones as well.

Dear reader, do not expect to find new knowledge here; perhaps a Work 'I' you have not tried and might want to put in practice today. What you will find in here is, above all, the same ancient teaching that Gurdjieff gathered and Ouspensky organized almost a century ago, and which is alive today in us, ordinary people trying to do the extraordinary: retrieve the miraculous present.

With Love,
Rolando Altamirano

Some men are changed by persuasion and others forget.
Argument steals the heart of one class, time of the other.

Socrates

Explaining Work Ideas to New Students

In our School we hold weekly meetings designed for new students. Our aim is to present them with the System ideas and explain how we put them into practice in our everyday life. We also share with them those ideas we practice which are not found in the Fourth Way literature.

In general, newer students already have some knowledge of the material we deal with. Yet in some cases, they are exposed to the System for the very first time.

As for those of us who have used the System for a long time, explaining the Work ideas to others allows us to see how much of what we explain is still theory for us, and how much is the result of our personal verification. We can find that out only through Self Remembering and impartial observation of our own machine.

However, every once in a while we observe I's that do not understand why the Work ideas have to constantly circulate, why we have to keep repeating the same things over and over. In this respect it is useful to remember that one of the features of the second state is our inability to be constantly attentive to the impressions we receive. In other words, we often drift into imagination while being exposed to the ideas. Also, in general, in the second state only one or two centers or parts of centers record what is being said or read at a given moment. That is probably one of the reasons why the same ideas have to be repeated over and over (both to those who just joined, and to those who have been in the School longer) until the part in us interested and able to do the Work, listens actively to the information and makes the aim to put it into practice.

From this point of view, we may say that simply attending a meeting, memorizing these ideas, or participating in any of our discussions does not guarantee that we will understand them. Therefore we have to keep an eye on the device that produces the illusion that simply because we have half heard, half read, half repeated and half memorized the Work ideas, we already understand them. If this were the case, even Gurdjieff would come on his knees begging us to teach him.

When we rewrite or repeat the System ideas, we do it as a way to remember and refocus on the Work, or to rearrange our thoughts so that we can apply them more often. Our meetings, discussions, publications and formal events are designed for this purpose.

As said before, an essential aspect of this matter is that the ideas we share and discuss in our gatherings (including this text) have to be put into practice. This way we keep producing new material for study and discussion and our meetings become useful for everyone.

Here are two ways to approach this practice.

The first one is to explore the ideas themselves. That is, we can take for example the idea of the deputy steward, or the idea of the difference between the second and the third state, or chief feature, and study it in our every day life with the aim to get direct knowledge of it: if we do so, we will come upon many questions and observations to share with other students.

The second one is to start from facts. That is, we can take simple facts of the machine's life and try to study them from the point of view of different Work ideas. For example we can take small I's such as: "I hate my boss", "The Teacher does not visit my center", "I am in love", "That student is stupid", "Wars affect everybody", or "I need to call my mom", and try to find out what feature or part of the machine generated them. Again, we will produce more material for study, and the System will become alive in us.

Needless to say that, without Self Remembering, direct study of this System is impossible. If Self Remembering is missing, sooner or later we will get bored of sitting around going over and over the same theoretical material. For when they do not lead to the awakening of higher centers, these ideas breed just another form of sleep.

There is no teaching... only recollection.

Socrates

When do we actually access our memory?

The following was written in response to the question of what is memory for a man number four, its nature and use; and how can we access that memory.

Our position as men number Four is paradoxical. When our consciousness is trapped in the machine we experience the being of a man number one, two or three, depending on which center takes the most space. Each center records in the moment those impressions that are of interest to it, and it files them away for future reference. When we sleep, all we are left with are fragmented memories of events. We remember only a color, a person's eyes, or "something someone said". Now, when we are fully aware of ourselves, we experience the being of a man number five: we are awake and present to what we are in the moment. Our moments of memory are related with the latter experience. What characterizes such moments is controlled attention and divided attention. If not remembering ourselves, we have to be at least working on the level of the steward; that is, making efforts to remember ourselves. There is no other way for the Self to create memory.

As men number four we have to constantly retrieve our center of gravity based in the Work, which is in the intellectual part of the emotional center: deputy steward or steward. This is the part of our machine that can help us remember the only thing we have to remember: **that we are asleep and wish to awaken**. Thus we can only access and make proper use of our memory when we are in the king of hearts, that is, when we are able to control our attention in the intellectual part of the emotional center.

As hinted before, the verification of higher states is also stored in the memory of lower centers. When a man number four sleeps, these memories are used by parts of the machine not interested in the Work. For example, false personality may use the very same collection of photographs we take of the machine in order to reassert itself by making them fit its imaginary picture. Thus, it is imperative that once we have made certain observations our own, once they have been recorded, our steward has to act upon them. A man number four keeps the memory of his observations in a specific file, with the aim to use them to work on himself.

At some point we are expected to have gathered enough information about ourselves in order to move beyond our mechanics. We cannot console ourselves with relative awakening. We have to constantly keep in mind why we are taking all these series of photographs, why we are collecting them, why we are interested in knowing certain aspects of our mechanics. Together with the study of our being as it is we must also study the way to transcend it. It is necessary that we study different techniques in order to attain that. If we verify that we lack the ability to remember this often enough, we have to ask for outside help. Help will eventually come, either from Influence C, our Teacher, other students, fate, the law of cause and effect or the law of accident.

So the idea of memory for a man number four is connected with the question. "Why am I here?" "Why did I take the trouble to be born?"

And the moral of this is: the more there is of mine, the less there is of yours.

Lewis Carroll

Payment

Ouspensky says there is only one word for the Work idea of "payment", and for lack of a better term we have to use it with different meanings from those we use in ordinary life.

We try to keep in mind that the Work is the study of a new language. When we deal with a term of the System that refers to a reality different from what we have so far experienced, we must first study the formatory apparatus' definition of it and see if it applies to the definition in the System. Different students have offered their own definitions of the term "payment", which have little or nothing to do with the System's idea. Here are a few observed in the Milan center:

- One is the Catholic notion that one has to pay because one has sinned or done something wrong in relation to God, the universe or oneself; that we were all born sinners and must pay for that through the sufferings of our lives.

- Another one is the superstitious fear that every time we experience something good we must pay for it with some kind of suffering.

- There is also the interpretation of the king of

clubs' idea of payment in the form of teaching payments and service to the School as a direct way of ensuring a place in paradise.

This text relates to the latter, that is, the idea of payment as our financial contributions or service to our Teacher and the School. I agree with Ouspensky that this is not exactly payment, but a way to help the organization of the School. The School is not an institution outside of us. We are the School, and it is up to us to keep it alive. At times we are in the position of playing roles such as that of center director, cook, member of the council, photographer, or dishwasher. Sometimes we are in the position to offer financial help for the development of new centers or of Apollo. But those are more or less circumstantial forms of help almost anyone can offer. When one fails to understand this, one runs the risk of getting one's conscience trapped in a role of service, or even of creating accounts towards our Teacher and the School, because the king of clubs feels it does not get anything out of it, except for the pathetic medal of reputation.

As soon as one sorts out mechanical I's in relation to payment one faces the task of living the question posed by Ouspensky's definition of this concept. Living the question means to find examples drawn from the context of one's own life. So, in order to understand the nature of payment, it is important to ask oneself the following questions:

- What do I want to get from the System and from

the School?
- What does the School offer?
- What do I have to do in order to get it?

Or start from the opposite end of the question:

- Did I get anything I did not have before I joined?
- What is it?
- How did I get it?
- Was it for free?

Ouspensky also states that no one but I can know what form of payment I need to make for what I wish to get. The way to make this subject practical is to try to remember my Self and observe the machine's reaction to that effort; for it is this very effort what unveils the expense.

What was that sorrow I was suffering in sleep?

Rumi

Sacrifice suffering

Suffering can be viewed as the stimulation of the negative halves of the emotional and the instinctive centers. I do not know whether there is such a thing as suffering in the moving center, since its negative half is rest, or in the intellectual center, since its negative half is "thinking no". As for the sex center and higher centers, they do not have negative halves, and what we usually experience as suffering related to the sex center might be sex energy leaking into the emotional or into the instinctive center. However, the longing or unfulfilled desire experienced when the sex center is active could be seen as a form of suffering created by that center.

It is also useful to distinguish between real suffering and imaginary or unnecessary suffering. Unnecessary suffering is the artificial stimulation of the negative half of the emotional center, through remembering some past episode or through eliciting some fear or frustration related to the future. When connected to an event in the present it is usually the result of a wrong attitude in relation to it, thus what suffers is personality. In short, imaginary or unnecessary suffering is related to false personality (the part in us that is not really our own) and not to essence. Real suffering is mainly related to a direct stimulus in the present, sometimes perceived by the emotional center, sometimes by the instinctive center, and it affects essence directly; for example, when one sprains one's ankle or feels shame for one's impertinent actions.

This writing deals with sacrifice, on one hand, as transformation of real suffering into presence; and on the other hand as renunciation of imaginary suffering; which is only a veil that prevents us from being present. Furthermore, it is clear that imaginary suffering cannot be transformed; thus the idea of "sacrifice" in this case means to find a quick way to just drop the matter and focus on the task of the moment.

There are different techniques to work with each type of sacrifice.

In order to sacrifice imaginary suffering we need to observe and separate from the part of the machine that believes it experiences the suffering. When we study this kind of suffering, we often observe it is the result of ignorance, laziness or lack of training in the intellectual center. There are a myriad of small events, past and present, which should not make us suffer, but the way we think about them causes us to suffer. In other words the way we relate to them stimulates the negative halves of centers. In this case what we need to sacrifice, drop or simply change is the way we think about events. We need to find more intelligent ways to ponder their significance.

Inner considering (identification with people) for

example, is a source of this kind of unnecessary suffering. Many people suffer because "My wife thinks I am fat", "I do all for my kids and they do not care", "Nobody understands me", "The Teacher does not give me attention", etc.

Other times we experience unnecessary suffering when images of some past real suffering appear in the memory of the emotional center. This is an indication that our attention has dropped to the level of the queens, since these memories are controlling it. Sacrifice of suffering in this case simply means to make the effort to divide our attention and focus on the task of the moment. For although this type of suffering does not take place in the present, it does take us out of the present, so the way to sacrifice it means also to simply focus on what we have to do in the moment. The effort is very similar to the one we make when we try to stop thoughts; although stopping thoughts in general is a more or less neutral endeavor.

Keep in mind that what makes the sacrifice difficult in this case is not the subject itself but identification with the subject.

In some cases, especially at very early stages of the Work, one may observe a wound in the emotional center that is still sore. Its slightest stimulation creates suffering, yet actual pain usually lasts very little. This type of suffering can be worked with as higher hydrogen circulating within the machine for a few seconds. When we divide attention while experiencing it we may experience the presence of higher centers, but just for as long as our will lasts. When we fail to divide attention, takes place a descending octave that can go on for hours or days on end. Even if we succeed in transforming the hydrogen given by this memory, we still have to sacrifice the I's that wish to keep suffering once the hydrogen has ceased to circulate.

Again, in earlier stages of the Work a sore memory may keep coming back to the surface of our awareness. Then it might be useful to intentionally study the past event from as many points of view as possible: which requires controlled attention in the emotional center. And once we figure out what bothers us about it, we have to make sure to move onto something else. Whether it is that some dear relation passed away, or that our essence was badly hurt, or that we made an irreversible mistake, we can always trace the issue back and study it from an objective point of view.

Careful study and acceptance of things as they happened is one of the best ways to sacrifice the residue of one's past real suffering. In this case sacrifice means to drop unnecessary extra suffering and make room for understanding.

There are other types of unnecessary suffering that come from small irritations in the present, which, due to negligence, we do not take the time and energy to transform and which tend to become bigger in time. Little irritations and tensions amongst people like, for example: partners, family members, workmates, and roommates; others due to circumstances such as the weather, the news, tiredness, hunger, traffic jams, flat tires, etc. All of them become the source of endless suffering if not worked with (sacrificed) in the moment. The technique here is very simple, separate from the part of the machine that suffers, let the hydrogen circulate.

I would approach sacrifice of real suffering a little differently. That is, in terms of transformation -an act of will similar to the transformation of negativity.

Real suffering is in the moment, and the first effort is to accept it. Whether it is that we just bumped our head, had a car accident, lost a friend, or were verbally abused, it does not make a difference: the first thing is to accept the fact that something just happened the way it happened and feel the hydrogen circulate as we divide attention.

Before we develop a steward, our essence spends most of its energies trying to fight back or escape suffering as much as possible. It takes much work and concentration to create and consolidate the attitude of accepting real suffering. Thus, part of the work connected to the acceptance of suffering is to control that device in the machine, which makes us act like a child who does not want to go to the doctor for fear of vaccinations.

Rodney Collin speaks of the necessity to not only refrain from running away from suffering, but to actually find ways to suffer voluntarily in order to develop will in the face of real suffering. A practical way to start working in this area is to introduce several forms of voluntary suffering during the day. Examples range from sitting in an uncomfortable position to bearing the unpleasant manifestations of people. Also, as we become familiar with our mechanical tendencies, we can turn many circumstances to our favor by accepting them as voluntary suffering. Say you feel a strong attraction towards someone else when you or they are already married; just turn it into voluntary suffering until it fades away. Because you know it will eventually fade away.

A great inner strength can be created through transformation of real suffering. Yet we still have to practice a lot and for a long time with small voluntary suffering, otherwise we will have no tools, nor will to face real suffering.

Imaginary or unnecessary suffering, as it has been implied before, does not exist, there is no use for it, so it is better to drop it, but the undisciplined child within us does not wish to do so. In the end it is a question of becoming more mature, more focused and sober.

Even though all hell should come upon us, we must be brave.

Silouan the Athonite

First Conscious Shock

During a discussion with friends I mentioned my verification of Ouspensky's affirmation that for a long time one has to get used to the unpleasantness of simply being able to apply the first conscious shock, because one is unable to apply the second conscious shock successfully. Someone then asked if this could be further explained with an actual example.

For several years the first conscious shock, or Self Remembering, is mainly connected to self-observation and self-study. This means that most of our efforts are focused on the development of a deputy steward. The actual creation of a deputy steward is a byproduct of the effort to remember our Self. We can recognize this aspect of our work by our increased ability to observe and analyze our mechanical manifestations from the point of view of the System. But for a long time this is limited to knowing what is going on in the moment, without having the will or the knowledge to act upon it.

Obviously some minor manifestations disappear as soon as the intelligence we call the deputy steward comes into being. We may consider them minor manifestations from the point of view of identification; that is, it is relatively easy to let go of subjects the machine is not intensely identified with. On the same premises we may consider certain mechanical manifestations as major, and they require a longer and more difficult work. The techniques are the same, the tools are the same, but due to the fact that identification is intense, the effort to apply the same tools seems greater. In other words Self Remembering or the effort to detach our identity from what we observe, when applied to a word exercise while at a meeting, or when our Teacher is around, seems relatively simple, it makes perfect sense. Yet when applied to the machine's favorite negative emotion, or to its chief weakness manifesting "when nobody is looking", it requires more consistent efforts.

When Ouspensky says, "one has to learn how to swim in calm waters", he partly means that we have to learn to separate from what we observe in a relatively neutral moment; for example, learning the difference between reading a book with divided attention or without it. Yet sooner or later, we must jump into the "open sea" and swim or drown. In other words we have to learn to separate and observe ourselves neutrally in extremely difficult moments, having to deal with great mechanical forces within us. Yet the focus of this activity is in the development of the "I" that observes; the "I" that separates from whatever mechanical event takes up space and time in the moment.

At some point in my work I began to apply the first

conscious shock in the middle of what I recognized then as the machine's favorite negative emotion. The first time I ever became aware of this mechanics (even when I had previously been photographed about it) I was surprised, but I fell asleep almost immediately after having seen it. Later on false personality did not really recognize it as a negative emotion, but as a general feeling that "something went wrong between me and the outside world". On the other hand, efforts to remember my Self in relation to word exercises, formal dinners, meetings, etc, kept going. But the idea to actively remember my Self in relation to the study of this particular form of negativity did not come to mind for a long time. Something like trying to be present when Dr. Jekyll was there, while being unaware of Mr. Hide.

Photographs kept coming my way, of course.

The possibility of change in relation to the event came when I started to accept photographs related to it. Next step was to verify its existence, which meant I had to make the aim to observe it. In the beginning I could not actually remember my Self in the middle of the negative emotion, but only shortly afterwards. What made me think of it as a main weakness in the moment was the strong sense of self-importance attached to the negative emotion itself. False personality felt Self Remembering and self-observation as some kind of intrusion into a taboo zone.

All I could figure *a posteriori* was that certain

circumstances triggered this emotion, and that I had to prepare myself to face it when the same circumstances came again. Preparation for this meant both, the creation of new attitudes in relation to the emotion and the aim to study it while being present to it. That of course implied the effort not to express the negative emotion. Many times I had the aim not to express it and ended up working with the negative emotions that come after failure. Yet other times my efforts went as far as trying not to run away from the circumstance that evoked it.

Anyway, one of the most interesting verifications is that we cannot observe a negative emotion unless we stop expressing it: as soon as we let go of the effort, the chance of studying it is gone. For a long time I focused on Self Remembering in relation to the study of this emotion. I did not expect to be able to change the nature of the negative experience. I simply had to learn to separate from what I was observing and to set aside for a while the study of ways to transform it. All I could do was focus on the process of creating my Self, not paying too much attention to the nature of the I's, but to the nature of the force I was trying to develop.

This is the unpleasant aspect of the first conscious shock, meaning the actual process of creating one's Self. One is trying to shift one's identity, by will, from a deeply rooted negative manifestation to one's true Self: the moment one stops making efforts one is back in hell: strangely enough **false personality prefers hell to effort.**

At this point I am still preparing for working on the second conscious shock or transformation of negativity in this case. I do not know enough about this machine. I am beginning to take a glimpse at the whole mechanical network that lies beneath a single negative emotion. The only thing I can say now is that I am beginning to see things differently, including this negative emotion. Certainly not for free, for in order to see things differently I need to make efforts to control my attention, and to consider every observation I make from the point of view of the Work.

Observing "I", deputy steward and steward are psychological stages that come as a result of a series of connected efforts. They are not mechanical in origin, but the moment one stops making efforts, they become part of our mechanics.

Reflect: is not the dreamer, sleeping or waking, one who likens similar things, puts the copy in the place of the real object?

Socrates

Lying

As men number four, we understand the idea of "Lying" differently from men number one two and three. We deal with "Lying" as a device used by false personality to make us believe we have full knowledge and control of our lives, and that all our actions, thoughts and emotions are understandable. False personality may make us believe that every time we speak about ourselves, we are trying to clarify or explain something. But when we wake up for a moment, we realize that most of the time false personality is interpreting its dreams, and what is most important, it is reinforcing the machine's imaginary picture. Therefore we view "Lying" as a sign of sleep.

An aim to verify this is to divide attention and observe the machine when we speak about ourselves. We need to learn to distinguish what part in us is speaking. Sometimes we may be truly sharing an impartial observation, other times we may be speaking from the level of attention of the deputy steward, trying to figure something out as we speak; yet other times false personality may only be trying to promote its imaginary picture.

In order to be able to tell the truth, we must be able

to know the truth, first in relation to ourselves –the truth about the external world is for now out of the question: all we have is opinions. We need to keep in mind that our perceptions of the outside world depend on our body type, alchemy, center of gravity, level of being, and level of awareness in the moment. This is another aspect of our study of lying. That is, the study of those devices which stand between our Self and the external world.

An essential aspect of the Work is to know ourselves, therefore to observe ourselves. Before we started working with the System, we did not have the possibility to really know ourselves. Instead, false personality used bits and pieces of different approaches to the understanding of our identity and behavior. Consequently we ended up with an imaginary idea of our identity and our behavior. It is interesting to note here that just as false personality used those bits and pieces to explain itself; it may now try to use the language of the System to do so.

The aim is to study how false personality does this as well.

Some of us have verified that in the passage from an observation to its classification we run the risk of lying; either because we do not know the System well enough, therefore we become students in the art of shooting in the dark, or because we do not take the time to carefully study ourselves in terms of the System. Studying ourselves requires developing attention both in the emotional and in the intellectual center. These parts have verified that for now the only accessible truth for us is the truth about ourselves, so it is within our interest to carefully study ourselves, and therefore neutralize lying.

Accepting photographs is crucial in this endeavor. When we receive a photograph, it is helpful to have the aim to write it down and use it as a point of reference for self-observation. (The photographs that the machine violently rejects are sometimes the most useful.) The truth about ourselves exists whether we are aware of it or not, and sometimes other people are aware of it, at least partially. The fact that we are asleep to it means we are covering it with some sort of lying.

In the Work we also make a distinction between knowing oneself and knowing one's Self, just like we make a distinction between a boat and the boatman.

Our possibilities to escape from lying are in the awakening of the higher emotional center. Therefore Self Remembering is our most immediate and effective way out, yet self-observation is already a great step in that direction.

As stated before, lying in relation to the world around us is obvious. Direct knowledge of the world is the function of higher intellectual center. Since we spend most of our time in the lower centers, our perception of the world is simply an interpretation of a reality still foreign to us.

Again, we have to study the device that stands between our Self and reality.

Who cares for you? Alice exclaimed; you're nothing but a pack of cards.

Lewis Carroll

Being Stuck In the Work

These thoughts were written in response to a question about the feeling of being stuck in the work, not knowing exactly where that feeling comes from.

There is a great difference between knowing one is stuck, and being stuck without knowing it. Just like there is a great difference between walking down a crowded street with one's eyes shut, and walking down the same street with one's eyes wide open.

Sometimes we experience the feeling of being stuck in relation to our role within the School or in life, or we feel stuck in a habit "that pleased us and then moved in for good[1]". Some other times we are stuck in a feature, yet other sometimes we associate being stuck to an interval in first or second line of work, etc...

The feeling of being stuck may be the faint voice of conscience trapped within one function or feature. Fortunately when we hear this voice it is already the beginning of movement. For other times we are indeed stuck, our friends notice it but we don't.

As I understand it now, our efforts to develop and control our attention in the emotional center may

---

1 Rainer Maria Rilke: *First Duino Elegy,* translated by D. Young

allow us to notice that we are stuck. Yet in order to escape that situation, it is necessary to make further efforts and sustain our attention longer. We need to carefully study the network behind the feeling of being stuck from the point of view of where it originates and how we can overcome it.

For example we may study the matter from the point of view of centers and parts of centers. We may ask ourselves what center is taking so much space in our everyday life that causes us to feel stuck. I would start with pen and paper: write down the I's verbatim as they express themselves in words, and then try to figure out which center or part of center might have produced them. When unable to figure it out, ask other students.

We can also try to approach the matter from the point of view of features -whether in essence or in personality is not important at the moment. The question to ask ourselves is what kind of laziness, stubbornness, lying or inertia prevents us from moving forward. Same technique, write down the I's and try to understand what gland might cause the machine to experience a certain mood and thus express that specific group of I's.

We can also study the matter from the point of view of having reached an interval in the octave of our evolution, and then use the tool of three lines of work. So the first thing to do is to figure out which of our three lines of work is in an interval, and then work on one of the other two in order to bridge it. As said before, the very fact of asking a question related to the problem is already an effort toward bridging the interval. Thus, we elicit second line, and our friends in the Work help us find different ways to refocus.

Anyway, feeling stuck gives us the opportunity to study certain "alignments of mechanics". Once this feeling subsides, or we move on to a different area of the Work, the opportunity to study this specific "alignment of mechanics" is gone. Additionally, as we try to figure out where the feeling of being stuck originates, we are working on the development of the deputy steward. If this is so, we are actually preparing the ground for that level of understanding and control we call the steward. Once we reach that level, we will already be familiar with the type of I's and features we are dealing with, and therefore we will be in the position to act more quickly on them.

You are the one who watches the game.

Rumi

The Need to create an Observer

This letter was written in response to a question about the usefulness of exploration of wounds and traumas inflicted upon essence, especially when we start to work on ourselves.

At the beginning first line of work involves the study of the System and the study of one's machine from the point of view of the System. That implies the development of an observing I; which means the development of attention in the intellectual and in the emotional center. The development of these parts of the machine requires aim and effort. In right order the magnetic center must yield to this aim and this effort.

If we are not able to sustain attention in higher parts of centers, lower parts will make use of the System language and try to "observe the machine" according to what interests them. An example is when we observe the machine from the level of attention of the queen of hearts and we come across a manifestation it disapproves. We then experience the impulse to quickly try to change it or get rid of it.

Also, when we get identified with our observations

it means we have stopped studying ourselves. The imperative effort is to retrieve our Self; and then resume our study. That is we have to divide our attention and then resume the study of the machine, for as Ouspensky said, "no work can be done in sleep".

It is also important to have an aim in relation to what we wish to study, because casual observations fall under the law of accident. They are regularly made by queens or jacks of centers and they just affect the mood of the machine. This is not what is meant by the "Observing I".

A way to approach this question is as the intentional study of essence and its mechanical tendencies and wounds. This study includes the understanding of where these mechanical tendencies and wounds stand from the point of view of awakening.

Our observations lead us to verify that, regardless of how well equipped personality might be, at some point in our life, essence stops experiencing the world by itself. Then an artificial device enters into play, a certain attitude that later develops into the machine's imaginary picture. Though it is relatively important to study the features of the imaginary picture, what we have to focus on is the force we create by separating from them.

It is essential, however, to observe and study carefully the wounds inflicted upon essence by the law of accident and the law of fate. And take them into consideration as we work on ourselves, for their effect on our lower centers may have some bearing on our vision of the Work, even if we do not realize it. Sometimes the wounds are so deep that we are not able to see them by ourselves. In this case we have to borrow or hire someone else's king of hearts and king of diamonds in order to be able to deal with them. This process is like bringing your car to a conscientious mechanic; and trying to figure out together with him what is wrong with it. Figuring that out takes time, but once we know it, we are half way out. We have to remember that we are "The Driver" who brings his car to the mechanic, not the broken car's device.

Information recorded in personality may change according to circumstances, yet information recorded in essence can only be changed with much work, knowledge and attention, for it has been crystallized in it through the direct experience of suffering.

When we suffer from a wounded knee, the wound is in the cellular body, and we are apt to realize it is only one aspect of ourselves that suffers. Yet when we suffer from a wounded essence, the wound is in the molecular body; that is why we are more prone to experience the wound as "ME". It is therefore important to understand that we are not the wounds; we are the **one** who observes them. Of course in the beginning this may seem a pure intellectual exercise, somehow unrelated to the wound. Yet effort-by-effort one's Self will manifest and know directly the meaning of "I am not the wound". Just as sometimes it manifests and realizes "I am not the headache."

Thus, our business is the development of a higher intelligence that has the purpose of studying the machine, whatever its condition; an "Observing I" separate from wounds, traumas or any other program running the machine.

The fathers suffered martyrdom, not in the outward sense, but in their conscience.

Peter of Damascus

Fear of Conscience

An aspect of the third state is that we become objective in relation to our mechanics. It means we become aware of whom we are as opposed to who we dream we are, or what we are supposed to be doing as opposed to what we imagine we are doing. If we were coherent with what we think, say and do, the third state would seem "the ecstasy". But most of us have verified that often we think one thing, say something else, and do something totally different; to become aware of this is something more like "the agony". As we awaken, we separate our identity from what we observe. When we maintain the effort to separate from our mechanics as we observe them, then "the agony and the ecstasy" become a reality. The agony is Rolando, the machine; the ecstasy is the Self, the "presence of third eye" as a separate entity.

Without the effort to separate from Rolando's manifestations, only it (the role, lower functions) exists immersed in the beatitude of its dreams, or the familiarity of its nightmares. Awakening of the Self will certainly disturb Rolando's imaginary existence. He will start thinking there must be something wrong with him etc... Rolando (lower functions, the role) is not meant to awaken; it is the Self who is meant to awaken and separate from the role.

We see the best of our friends leave the School right at the moment when they start to have flashes of conscience, when they start to see themselves, but fail to detach their identity from what they see. Awakening is there, within grasp, but there is nothing in them that wants it.

Some of us remember how a moment of conscience unveils, in one split second, the apparently unbearable reality of the multiplicity of I's, and how quickly a tremendous force brings us back to sleep.

In our case, this same moment of truth about us may come after five, ten, or twenty years of being in the School. And sometimes it comes accompanied with the sense of time wasted, time spent under the illusion that we are going to paradise one by one, effortlessly. These I's come from the queen of hearts, and we separate from them. The point is to remember that we are not what we observe. We are the observer. Eventually we become that which is present, again and again.

To be or not to be is not a question for us; we have chosen to be.

Athena warned Perseus never to look at Medusa directly, but only at her reflection, and presented him with a brightly polished shield.

Anonymous

Buffers

In a flash of conscience we realize what it means to have been cast upon a particular machine and not on any other. Many possibilities open for us then. But we have to make the effort to remember what we saw during this temporary look into the fourth dimension, and keep it in mind for future work. Additionally, we need to observe the buffers false personality uses to shut up conscience right after we have a glimpse of it. That is, *"the impenetrable barriers"* which keep us from seeing the contradictory nature of our own feelings and thoughts.

In the beginning we do not have the being to shed light on buffers and remove them at will; therefore we have to find indirect ways to break through them.

Buffers have to be eliminated one step at a time and in an intelligent way, because the intelligence within the machine, the king of clubs, controls them. It has been pointed out that if buffers are removed in an unprepared person his or her psychological balance would be upset. That is why in ordinary life false personality makes sure this does not happen.

A very useful tool to remove buffers indirectly and in an organized way is to become actively interested in getting information about our mechanics. Remembering that Medusa can only be looked at through a reflection, but never directly in the eyes, we keep an "I" open to photographs we get from Robert, other students, and even life people. Life people can be very useful if we manage to decode what they are trying to tell us not only through their comments, but also through their attitudes towards us.

In order to succeed in this endeavor it is necessary to not inner consider people who offer us their opinion about our mechanical behavior. Plutarch advises us to even take advantage of our enemies' judgment of our actions, as they are very actively interested in pointing out our weaknesses correctly.

Sometimes we are lucky to get photographs from Robert or from a student who is more awake than us in the moment. Usually these photographs are given from the king of hearts. In this case our own king of hearts becomes active, and we can feel that these photographs are meant to help us awaken. In this case we are more likely to wish to verify what we hear.

When we make the study and control of our mechanics a permanent aim, we can use any piece of information we receive from all people around us, whether or not they are students.

Finally, every time we break through a buffer we have

to accept the machine's contradictions and separate our identity from them. We know that the machine produces many different I's, often contradictory. We also know that we are neither the machine nor the I's.

Breaking through a buffer releases a fair amount of higher hydrogen; the effort to separate from what we see puts us in direct contact with our true Self.

Now, here, you see, it takes all the running you can do, to keep in the same place. If you want to get somewhere else you must run at least twice as fast!

Lewis Carroll

When traveling through centers

This article was written shortly before Robert started leading meetings around the world.

We have to be careful not to confuse traveling within the body of the School with traveling around the world. Although they can be one and the same experience, this is only true when we keep in mind the nature and aims of the School. When we sleep, we are just cellular bodies pulled and hauled by the cosmic forces at work within a given moment. The same applies when we travel to different cities in order to meet students and we fail to keep in mind the School's nature and aims.

Robert travels through the world for specific reasons, and as he travels, he summons his School. His students come to him wherever he is. He says that his journeys to Italy are mainly first line of work. Indeed, when he comes here, he usually sees just a limited number of students and has little or no contact with the centers here. As for third line, he keeps visiting art galleries, museums, gardens and stores, looking for impressions to add to the beauty and culture of Apollo and his students. Of course it is good to remember that he keeps teaching day by day, in a direct way, a train of younger students.

When playing the role of traveling teacher or support student, the focus of the trip is on second and third line. The main task is to spend as much time as possible with students, and create situations that will enable the participants not only to discuss Work ideas and their practice but to try to be present as well. In general, whenever we take part in a School event with a specific role, given either by the teacher or by the organization of the School, chances are that interaction with students will remain on a higher level of attention. Conversation and general attitudes in relation to other students will be of a finer quality, the aim and purpose of our meeting will be to remind each other of the higher right in the moment, to remind each other to be present.

However, sometimes we travel to other cities for reasons not necessarily connected with the actual activities of a center. Sometimes we travel for work, other times in order to nourish our essence (or first line of work) then meeting students is not necessarily the main reason why we travel to a specific place. In this case we have to be creative in finding ways to keep the work alive amongst us as we casually meet over lunch or dinner, or a stroll down the avenue of the hotel where we stay.

I have observed several I's that act as a denying force while trying to meet students when I travel for reasons not connected to an activity of the School. These I's are produced by the instinctive center and, although in life some of them might be useful, in our School they diminish our possibilities to work on second and third line of work.

Laziness: This starts to happen after a few years in the School. As the machine gets older, it tends to gravitate exclusively towards its friends, favorite students, or those types and circumstances it feels more comfortable with. It does not wish to invest energy in new acquaintances.

Fear: As years go by, the instinctive center develops a shield that prevents certain types from coming close: "I do not know who those people are", it says.

Accounts: False personality uses a device in the instinctive center meant to protect the machine to protect itself from other students. It wants to isolate us in order to defeat our work.

Imagination related to gossip: After hearing information about someone, especially of negative nature, the instinctive center becomes alert when they are around.

Vanity or competition: False personality tries to introduce in conversations certain topics that enable it to display its curriculum within the Fellowship. "Who's been in the School longer, who's been a traveling teacher, talked recently to Robert or read and memorized more work books etc." The presence of a young-enough-member of the opposite sex might trigger this.

Feminine dominance: Other times, when planning

to visit centers, false personality would wish to visit newer centers where it can display its knowledge of the System and feel liked and, or respected in return.

Of course with attitudes and I's like these, School on earth is merely an illusion.

In general, newer centers or centers with newer students are more enthusiastic about meeting just any student coming from another country. Like kids, they are more ready, willing and able to make use of the possibilities provided by the School. Newer students are generally positive and open; they are live reminders of the great opportunity we were given when we met the School.

Yet as centers naturally grow older, mechanical tendencies start to develop amongst the students in each center and this makes our interactions somewhat difficult. As a new student one is more willing to risk and experiment, yet as one's time in the School ticks away, the machine starts to develop I's similar to the ones mentioned above. Also, sometimes little groups and couples start to form, charismatic characters take space, and visitors are sometimes seen as outsiders. This seems to be the manifestation of a law: the instinctive center always usurps our undertakings, marking its territory in every situation.

This process is very similar to what happens when one creates a garden. Once it is finished, weeds start growing day after day. Weeding is a less creative and more tedious job than planning or laying it out, but it has to be done, otherwise the garden is bound to become a jungle again. It is important to find a way to stop this descending octave once we become aware of it.

Here in the Milan centre we are pretty much used to traveling students and visitors, since it is a central point both for Europe and for the School in terms of circulation. There is a definite infrastructure to welcome them and give them attention, even when they come unexpectedly. Yet sometimes we travel to a centre where the lack of an infrastructure to welcome and take care of traveling students, puts additional pressure on their instinctive center.

Then creativity means to find ways to meet. For example last time we visited a centre unexpectedly, students there were very kind and open to make the necessary arrangements for us to get to know the city and have a place to rest for the night. Since staying overnight was not possible at their place, after dinner we went to their flat for a glass of wine. It was an inspiring experience to briefly look into the life of men number four we had never met before, and see the Work taking place under different circumstances than the ones we are used to. Age, credentials or nationality did not count: connection between students takes place on a higher, invisible realm. **The School is like a fragrance**. We can only recognize it through certain subtle details, not different from what we see in ordinary life.

One thing I have discovered is that the more intentionally we arrange our meeting with students, the more opportunities to be present arise for all of the participants. For example, sometimes it is more useful to prepare a dinner at a student's home than to go out to a restaurant. Also, when dining, it is best to make and keep the aim to have one single subject of conversation.

It is also useful to have a learning attitude when talking to a student we have never met before, and trust that he or she will have something to share about the Work we might have not considered so far. In any case, it is good to have the aim to refrain from speaking too much (unless asked directly) or in a patronizing way about the System, and to remain open and attentive to what friends wish to share with us. Always keep a watchful "I" on chief feature.

The machine does not like to have an aim when meeting students. Meeting students just for the sake of meeting is not the best aim. When we start to get acquainted with the nature and form of the School, this might suffice. Yet after a while it is better to have an aim when we meet another student. **People who work on themselves are precious beings, hard to find in the desert of life**, we cannot waste our time and theirs simply meeting to *"pour the void into the nothing"*. Even if we happen to meet someone on the street, we have to be ready to realize the highest possibilities in the moment. That takes being present and developing certain sensitivity. We do not need to wait until we are asked to lead an event, or meet Robert, or receive a shock from Higher Forces, or attend a formal dinner. We need to keep finding ways to evoke Presence in every situation.

Without Presence, we are simply ordinary people traveling around the world in order to meet those we mechanically enjoy to be with, or to visit a museum, follow our partner, take certain impressions, accept a job offer, visit our family etc... (We really are no more than that, when we simply go places in deep sleep). Most of us agree with Robert when he says that the difference between people we call "life" and us is *"only when we make the effort to shed light on life itself."*

We all have met life people who are very mature, intelligent, fun, creative and kind. Yet, however remarkable these people might be, it is quite clear they lack something. Robert's assertion that they "do not have our luck" is recognizable. They lack the secret students working on themselves retrieve over and over. On the other hand, when we as students cease to look for, and remind each other of that precious secret we have received through the School, we fall way down below the level of these normal people we call "life".

Apollo itself, without the effort to be present would be just a little village in the middle of nowhere, a caricature of European magnificence. Yet because of the concentrated effort of students, Apollo surpasses any magnificence, past and present.

Higher centers understand directly that one's life is an illusion (traveling included) they do not need death to prove that. It is good to remember that lower centers are limited by their nature, their field of interest and perception, thus for them it is necessary to have clear points of reference when traveling. So it is understandable to sometimes wish to visit friends and family in different parts of the world, or to move to another city because the sex center feels the impulse to mate: that is also available within the Fellowship of Friends. But when we fail to understand the meaning of the School from higher centers and higher parts of centers, we are in a worse position than people who do not have the luck of knowing about Self Remembering, about connection to Higher Forces, about the real possibility to transcend organic life on earth.

Because of everything and not in spite of it we continue our ascent.

Robert Burton

After Girard's Stroke

Shocks act on centers but not on consciousness. In some cases they may cause higher centers to awaken for a period of time, when lower centers do not have the necessary information that allows them to react. Yet higher centers can only remain awake by continuous effort: by will in the moment. I agree with Ouspensky who stated that a shock collects energy for a certain amount of time; yet I also acknowledge the need to act by will on this energy before it goes away, because it will eventually go away.

I remember, for example, the first time I was able to make a conscious effort after Robert threw a piece of bread across the table at a dinner -we all have seen him provide that and similar shocks a number of times. This time the bread had not reached the person it was intended to, and hit the piano placed in the middle of the Galleria living room. I suddenly found myself charged with what I now describe as Higher Hydrogens, and felt the experience slowly fading away as Robert went on saying "This is your **Self**". I made the effort to relax and experience my Self as it dispelled the I's circulating at the moment, yet this effort did not last long. A few moments after, I recorded the experience as follows: "This shock did not produce effort, it only created an opportunity, but it did not create will. Ouspensky is right; a shock does not replace effort."

Shocks can come from different sources, some may be produced by mechanical laws, such as the law of cause and effect or the law of accident; some may come from a more conscious source, such as those intentionally produced by one who is more awake, by the Teacher or by Influence C. Yet there is a different type of shock which remains the only one in relation to awakening which I as an individual, can and must produce actively and continuously, the first conscious shock: Self-remembering. That specific shock to evoke my Self in the moment is within reach every three seconds. No bread flying across the table, nor the death or misfortune of the best of my kin will replace that. Is it not this what Robert means when he says: "I receive a shock every three seconds"? Does he not mean one has to be continuously making an effort?

According to my present understanding, some of the I's produced by the machine once the energy of a shock has waned can open the door to a new level of understanding or to a new way of working on oneself. Other I's instead, are meant to dwell on a purely mechanical level, and if not checked they can slow us down and even undermine our work.

I call some shocks negative because they stimulate the negative halves of centers. The news about Girard

Haven's[2] brain stroke for example, was one of these. Once the energy collected by this shock waned, a series of negative I's started to circulate. I will just mention the ones that, although seemingly legitimate, were likely to undermine my work. I will also mention others similar to those described by some of the students who shared their own reactions to the same shock.

It may be useful to mention that in order to accomplish this study, it has been necessary to work on separating from the I's and see them as such, as if I were studying someone else's response to the shock. The first effort is to make them a subject of study instead of identification.

This specific group of I's came by storm, and their speed and intensity made me realize they originated in the negative half of the queen of hearts. They sounded pretty much like this: "What if Girard dies? What will happen to the School when Robert dies? What if Girard is out of circulation? Many people still depend on him and Robert. What will we do then?"

Obviously these I's reveal the self-centered attitude of the machine. They are very similar to what some people feel when they fear their parents might die. They really do not show interest in relation to the trial Girard is going through but are exclusively concerned with the implications for them. I see that these I's feel legitimately real, just as anything affecting essence feels legitimate. Yet keep in mind that an immature

---

2   A prominent student of our School

essence feels someone always needs to be there to take care of it. Yet we work with the idea of carefully pushing essence beyond its level of being.

Now Girard's and Robert's work and presence have become a vital point of reference for people with a young essence in the School, a source of inspiration and guidance for many others, consequently, the loss of either of them will not be an easy shock to transform (It will be difficult for everyone anyway). But the way we work with what now presents itself as a potential reality, will determine how we, both as individuals and as a School, will be able to manage without the influence of these men.

A sound way to approach this matter is to study the way Rodney Collin, Plato or the Apostles worked with the trials and physical disappearance of their teachers: they just kept going from the point where their teachers' roles ended and they worked according to their "own sweet skill". I also found it good to remember Robert's words -as I recall reading in an old Journal: "A teacher does not have to be present to be teaching. This is a misconception students have."[3]

Here is an alternative which came to my mind as I was trying to figure a way to neutralize the group of I's in question. I remember back in '84 there was a student whom the Teacher said was a man number five. He was a very kind, collected and educated

3 *Renaissance Journal* 09/13/76

person, a real point of reference for many of us. His decision to leave the School taking along with him a number of students created a big shock for every one at Apollo (then Renaissance). There was a deep feeling of tragedy, loss and confusion amongst those of us who decided not to follow him. I personally saw it as a full-size folly on his side. For a few days we wondered what was going to happen next.

I remember talking to Girard about how to work with the issue. Amongst the many thoughts and work ideas we explored during that conversation, he shared a couple of work I's that I found worth trying. As I remember he said:

"You and I are asleep. The only possible thing we may attempt is to awaken. In our sleep, we even run the risk of being misled without realizing it. That is why to awaken is the most imperative thing. Our efforts in that direction cannot rely on anybody else's."

The fact that he said "you and I are asleep" instead of "Man is a sleeping machine" helped me realize that he knew he was asleep, and that he understood very well what that meant; now he was inviting me to realize the same for myself. So, for both of us the only thing to focus on was awakening. And he went on with his aim and efforts, independently from the fact that someone else had made it, or was gone. Ten years later Robert said that Girard himself was a man number five. Both of us had gone through the same Shock back in '84, and have been in the School ever since. As for myself, although I am positively more awake than before I started to remember my Self today I do not claim that I am permanently awake.

The next thing to consider is the way Girard is dealing with his new trial, and those of us who follow his messages can verify that he simply keeps working in the moment, regardless of his bodily condition, and he keeps sharing with us the fruits of his labor. I believe this is a more objective and profitable way to look at him; that is as a man number five or not, who just keeps making efforts regardless of circumstances.

Another aspect of this group of I's is the need to look for a guide to follow, or some superhuman being that provides insight from a higher realm. That is certainly a limiting factor for anyone wishing to awaken. Robert often says that Higher Forces do not wish any followers, and many of us might have verified that the very nature of consciousness discards that possibility. Robert carefully withdraws his influence from students who have been close to him and lets them become their own third force. He invites every one of us to work alone. Anyway, it is common sense that any man aiming to become a part of the conscious aspects of the ray of creation cannot expect to be breastfed understanding for ever, he has to gain it for himself though trial and toil; just as Girard is doing right now.

Now this shock has been strong enough to remind me of the fact that all of us, Girard and Robert included, depend on Higher Forces. It is them who are bringing us into being; they are our true parents and mentors. We are part of their plan, a plan greater than any of us can conceive. We are all children in the hands of Higher Forces, and we are grateful for that.

It is very hard to accept the fact that I do not know anything about Girard's play itself. All I know is that conscious beings experience a lot of friction throughout their lifetime, and that in order to pass from one stage of their evolution to the next they have to transform great suffering. The creation of a conscious being does not depend on mechanical laws - such as the law of feminine dominance- his birth in the molecular and or electronic world depends on higher principles and laws, his trials and disappearance from the cellular world are planned according to the degree of perfection he is meant to achieve. I have no idea of what I will have to transform once I reach that stage. For now it should be enough to be able to witness, record and expect the unexpected.

Finally, there is also the more immediate, householder related aspect of Girard's condition: He is a friend of ours who now requires special care and help with specific practical matters, such as hospital bills and various octaves. This is another practical way of relating to the issue, which helps us separate from the machine's personal interests and views about it.

So once we have sorted out the mechanical reactions to the initial shock, we may ask ourselves whether we may be of any practical use to Girard. Otherwise, for now it will suffice to keep working steadily on first second and third line of work, wherever we are, and accept the will of Higher Forces.

If some object could be found such that it both is and at the same time is not, that object would lie between the perfectly real and the perfectly unreal.

Socrates

Lost Information

Some of the information Robert passes on to us or that arrives to us by means of daily cards[4] and word of mouth, remains in the memory of the intellectual and emotional center simply because it is shocking, but not necessarily because it is understood or verifiable. On the other hand, some of the information we personally hear him say is impossible to verify and, although it is useful to keep it in mind, we cannot afford to make a dogma out of it. We can only approach it from a theoretical point of view.

When dealing with information coming from a conscious source, most times we are unaware of the context where it was formulated. Some of us have verified that when Robert says something at a dinner, he speaks primarily to the people who are present. Sometimes he communicates specific information to one particular person; other times he asks a student to make a daily card of something he says in order to share it outside that specific context.

Daily cards travel around the School and, following

4 Every day of the year students at Apollo receive a card with a quotation, an insight from the Teacher. Students around the world receive it through the Internet.

mechanical laws, they fall like seeds in many different places; unfortunately they do not always fall on fertile soil. When pondered in the second state, the words of a conscious being inevitably become B influence, and eventually A influence, it is up to us not to let this happen. When higher centers or at least higher parts of centers are not active, our Teacher's words become diluted or interpreted by lower parts of centers. Again, when not pursued through effort and practice, or through careful consideration, instructions from a conscious source are meant to become blind religion, food for argument, superstition, speculation or other forms of sleep. Our Teacher has nothing to do with this, for that manifestation of the law of accident is not under the control of a conscious being.

The hero knows not how to arrive there by himself alone; he has to seek the help and guidance from Higher Forces.

Russian Fairy Tale

Influence C

One of the differences between Influence C and influence B is that influence B is mainly a record of what once was Influence C. Only Influence C can provide every individual with the right circumstances for his or her evolution. Unless we establish a connection with this influence that is conscious in origin and in action, our efforts to awaken will prove fruitless. Although our Teacher does not state that he is influence C for us, when we are in a higher state we recognize that he lives permanently in that state which we are constantly trying to retrieve. We also recognize his love and patience as he creates the conditions for us to attain his level of being.

Most of us have also verified Influence C on a higher scale, that is, as the intelligence that has brought us together to create our School. We refer to it as Higher Forces. Our main verification is that through their influence, each of us is provided with the necessary conditions which best help us work on ourselves according to our level of being, center of gravity and features.

Common sense helps us understand that with influence B, there is no connection between us individuals and a conscious source. Nevertheless influence B is safer for the machine because it does not imply any serious work on oneself. Every time we deal with I's interested in B influence, in reality we deal with the remnants of our magnetic center, or with laziness: the king of clubs trying to postpone real work.

We must focus on what brought us here, Influence C. Once we are certain that we have come in contact with an influence coming from a higher world, our responsibility and urgency is to remain connected to them. We can achieve this through the awakening of higher centers only.

Gurdjieff, Ouspensky and Rodney Collin referred to Influence C primarily as the influence of a more developed man over a less developed man. Robert refers to Influence C at a higher level, that is, a School Higher than our own working with us. I see him as a bridge between them and men number four; most of us have verified this fact, some are in the process.

Some of us receive Robert's direct conscious influence and verify that it mainly means work. There is no gratification for the machine in our interactions with our conscious Teacher. Of course false personality feels safer "using information to enhance one's evolution" that comes from a conscious being whose role has been completed. Thus false personality feels the righteous heir to their work, and it does not have to suffer the actual living Teacher.

One of Robert's and Higher Forces' aims is to help

our presence emerge. In order to accomplish this they create special conditions and shocks. Regardless of the nature of these conditions and shocks, the machine will always offer resistance to work with them.

False personality thinks it can choose this or that School or Teacher, it thinks it can awaken for itself, get conscious, go home and tell everybody. It does not know that in order to awaken one has to be chosen from a higher realm for a specific purpose. If one is meant to become a part of the conscious aspects of the ray of creation, one has to be ready to put one's Self at the service of Higher Forces and follow their plan, which is on a scale higher than the little existence of the machine. Just like Robert and his inner circle serve Higher Forces. So we must elicit, and serve the higher in one another, thus our lives become less and less personal, more universal.

Some of us have verified that our School has a definite task to perform while it is active, that is the creation of Apollo, the pursuit of Plato's Ideal State. As we start to understand this idea, we move towards the inner circle of our School and we have no time to loose pondering the significance of alternatives, nor do we have the aim to worry about those who are still caught up in A or B influence. We simply are too busy to get distracted; distractions exist where there is oblivion, or lack of an aim.

I am sorry about the pain, but that is the nature of evolution.
                                                            Robert Burton

Transformation

In the second state, "understanding" is limited to the center that prevails in the moment, that is probably why we sometimes say that we have an "emotional understanding" of what it means to transform suffering, yet we realize we are not using this tool efficiently enough. In order to increase understanding and therefore work more efficiently on transformation, the intellectual center has to be engaged. That way it is possible to find out for sure when we are transforming and when we are not transforming suffering. False personality does not bother thinking about it. It prefers to leave things vague and is satisfied with relative understanding.

In my perception, transformation does not just mean to use shocks as alarm clocks for Self-Remembering. Self-Remembering is the first conscious shock, and transformation is the second conscious shock. The second conscious shock may be practicable only after we have applied the first conscious shock frequently enough and long enough. In other words, in order to be able to transform real suffering, we first need to determine whether or not suffering is real. That is whether it is the actual stimulation of the negative halves of centers in the moment or the result of ignorance, poor thinking or lack of understanding; most of the times suffering is a result of the latter. One can verify this by simply asking oneself the following questions:

Is suffering here right now?

What part of the machine is suffering -about what?

How long is this supposed to last?

Imaginary suffering can go on for days, weeks and months on end, depending on what is stronger, our steward or the machine's tendency to procrastinate. In comparison, real suffering lasts very little, and as mentioned above, it takes place in the present.

At times, once real suffering has ended, the machine creates unnecessary suffering by bringing the subject to mind over and over. Both, unnecessary and imaginary suffering, have to be disposed of by using the same techniques we use for staying out of imagination (the looking exercise, or simply to do what has to be done in the moment, etc). In some persistent occasions it is necessary to intentionally change our attitude in relation to what makes the machine suffer, thus we need to study the matter deeper (without wasting too much time on it). Life psychology also deals with getting rid of imaginary suffering, in fact it is meant to help people experience a more balanced second state.

Rodney Collin explained to us that real suffering fixes in us whatever attitude we have as we experience it. Thus when we fail to understand the role of real suffering in our evolution, not only it gets wasted, but it fixes in us negative emotions such as resentment, self-pity or anger.

Most of the suffering we "share" with the rest of humanity, like death of close ones, illness, emotional wounds, accidents etc, is called involuntary suffering. We did not ask for it, it always feels unexpected. Yet we turn it into voluntary suffering by accepting it and creating the right attitude towards it. Using common sense every time we question that which makes the machine suffer will help us create the right attitude to transform it in the moment.

Transformation of suffering is an act of will, as is Self Remembering. Paradoxically, one's Self emerges as one transforms suffering and only one's Self is capable of transformation. The techniques used are very similar to the techniques used to transform negative emotions. For example not to express any I's and just observe them as they wonder through the mind, not to speak to others about it, stop thoughts, accept suffering... Girard's definition is "separation of suffering in a way that one can experience it freely and without negativity". That means we are not what suffers, but we are present to it.

It is useful to remember the silent nature of the inner force we develop, one effort at a time, which allows us to face real suffering, because real suffering really hurts (imaginary suffering is somewhat comfy). It is also useful to keep in mind that transforming suffering does not mean to transform the experience itself, but to create and reassert one's Self through it. That implies to become stronger and more sober instead of identifying with it.

Although suffering is not a negative emotion, identification with real or involuntary suffering can produce a negative emotion that may even disguise itself as transformation. Christianity's "Mea Culpa" approach to suffering is a good example, and a great number of essences in our School have been "marinated" in that religion.

It has been said that Self Remembering is the first conscious shock, transformation of suffering, as well as transformation of negative emotions, is the second conscious shock. And that before we can apply the second conscious shock, we have to have gathered, through the first conscious shock, enough material related to what we are trying to transform. In other words before we can transform suffering successfully we have to learn to remember our Self in relation to the above-mentioned subjects. That is, distinguish real from imaginary suffering, or voluntary from involuntary suffering, neutralize the I's that wish to escape from real suffering, understand what part of the machine experiences suffering. Thus, one should study all the instances in which the machine thinks it is suffering and make a distinction between them.

We may be surprised to realize that most of our suffering will have to be filed under "imaginary" or "useless".

A parallel effort is the introduction of voluntary suffering in a small scale on a regular basis. There are many exercises in this area that can help us study the nature of real suffering, and study intentional ways to work with it. That way, when we experience major and minor shocks or unexpected real suffering, we will have developed the strength to transform them.

Finally, the point is to focus on the creation of one's Self, since the nature and intensity of suffering depend on forces beyond our control. When the Self is present, it does not suffer on the same scale of the machine; its suffering might be simply to witness the inevitability of the laws that govern the machine. Is this not the agony and the ecstasy?

We act a play on the chess board of existence.

Omar Khayyam

The Play

In the School we work with trying to verify the theory that The Fellowship of Friends is a "Play" written by Higher Forces. The play is a series of events and circumstances designed for ascending souls to move upward in their evolution. Thus, the life of every one of us is seen from the point of view of a "role" within the play of the Fellowship. Additionally, the lifetime of each individual is seen as a play itself, presenting a certain degree of difficulty for an ascending soul to work with in order to perfect itself. In case it fails to move on, it becomes more and more entangled in the illusions of human existence.

The following considerations are presented as a practical approach to this theory.

It is possible to read part of the script in our play; but in order to read it we have to be awake. The moment we fall asleep, the theory of the "Play" becomes just a dream or a topic of conversation over a cup of coffee.

We have full but not free access to any information regarding the role we happen to play. The tools we are given for this purpose are self-observation and Self Remembering. We are also given a System that helps us classify our observations in relation to a greater whole. When we start observing the machine we verify, amongst other things, our own role's center of gravity and body type. We also recognize that our particular role has a certain amount of knowledge, a certain behavior, definite tendencies -some we may call evolutionary, some devolutionary. We can also study the cultural and social context that produced our role's programming. Finally, we can observe its behavior and influence (conscious and mechanical) within the context of the School.

A greater part of first line of work is the careful study of our role, the main reason of this being to find ways of escaping it, not as a means to find a sense of identity. As a matter of fact, the way to escape our role is to keep our identity separate from its manifestations as we observe them. Since the process of self-study and self-observation is not a pleasant one, separation of our identity from what we observe is of vital importance. This is an aspect of Self Remembering.

Sometimes we experience a flash of conscience and we are able to see for a moment the long body of our role. We see, for example in this case, Rolando as he has been from the moment he was produced until the present. Then all our previous observations and their classification according to the possibility of escaping make perfect sense. In a flash of conscience we are able to realize what it means to have been cast upon one particular machine and not on any other: a great opportunity opens for us then. We must however; act on this opportunity as soon as possible before it falls away from our field of awareness, otherwise false personality might take over and make us forget about it.

Rolando represents a certain type of prison, certain set of features, of weaknesses that I, the Self, have to experience, learn to recognize and separate from. Rolando is a role that produces a certain illusion, a certain way of interpreting reality. Only I get to study my way out of Rolando, if I were trapped within some other role I would have to study what that role entails in order to escape it.

The theory of nine lifetimes implies the Self has been before. The System and the School are designed to help the Self remember to be awake. When I awake within Rolando, the task of the moment becomes very clear. It leaves no space to think about any other lifetime but this one, I get to play Rolando this one time only, and I realize that my time, and no one else's, keeps ticking away.

The just man does not permit the several elements within him to interfere with one another or any of them to do the work of others.

Socrates

Wrong Work of Centers

This morning, as I was thinking about a certain subject, I noticed that at some point the quality of my thoughts began to change. The subject matter was still the same but the way I related to it was changing. I stopped thoughts, and then realized that the machine was experiencing a slight discomfort, a clear general sensation of unease that had been there for a while and had stayed even after I stopped thinking. I tried to listen to the voice of the instinctive center and suddenly the "I" appeared, "I had too much coffee".

The instinctive center had become active while I was thinking, so the actual intellectual process stopped and only the illusion of it remained. That is, in my mind there were I's related to the subject, but they were not thoughts. Once the instinctive center became active, the subject was approached from the point of view of the machine's comfort and well being, not from the point of view of studying the subject itself.

This is an example of wrong work of centers.

Thinking is a neutral process that takes place in the intellectual center. It is designed to contemplate the nature and meaning of a given subject, without necessarily having an opinion about it. Thinking is linear, it deals with one subject at a time and it often ends in wonder. Yet we may observe that every time we try to think other centers and parts of centers produce opinions on the subject, depending on their field of interest; therefore they have to be kept in perspective. Sometimes they might be useful, yet other times they might be irrelevant to the subject we are dealing with.

Say, for example, we read an angle or a question in the Apollo Discussion List[5]. Right work would be first of all, to try to understand what the writer is saying: simply that. For this purpose we have to control our attention, without letting it drop to the level of the queens or the jacks, while reading the information. This is the task of kings of centers.

It is also necessary to observe and separate from other parts of the machine that may produce I's as we read. For example sometimes the sex center influences our attitude towards the writer. Other times formatory mind likes to browse through the Discussion list and see who is saying the right thing and who is saying the wrong thing, thus producing opposite I's. Yet other times we have an account with the writer, or heard and promoted gossip about them. In these cases a proper reading is impossible.

---

5   The Apollo Discussion list used to be a means for Students to communicate through the Internet. It has now been discontinued.

It may well be that, after carefully reading a contribution, we still do not understand (or as false personality puts it, "disagree with") some of the information contained in it. Then we have the right to ask for clarifications so that we put ourselves in the position to understand it.

If we decide to offer an angle in the Discussion, again we have to sustain attention, both in the intellectual and in the emotional center throughout the process of writing. This is necessary in order to know what to say, what not to say, and to find the best and more polite way to express it. As I understand it now, the aim of our Meetings, Dinners, Forum and Apollo Discussion list, is to provide insight in order to help one another work more efficiently.

When we write from the jacks or the queens, we are shooting in the dark more than anything else. We might still think or feel we are right, but the feeling of being right is a feature of our sleep; just as self-righteousness is a feature in most people who practice any religion or pursue any spiritual way.

Finally, Self Remembering will help us separate from that part of the machine, which, like a worm, is trying to express itself over and over. I remember once, while talking to Girard about writing a letter to another student, as I recall he said:

"Edit your letter till your message becomes clean."

"Clean from what?" I said.

"Clean from chief feature, imagination, the expression of negativity ..."

Needless to say that editing is possible only through divided attention.

God selects His own instruments and sometimes they are queer ones.

Abraham Lincoln

Sense of Injustice

A few months ago I saw a documentary on lions where they show a young male overtaking an older one's herd. After beating his opponent and chasing him away from the conquered territory, he goes on to kill the lioness' cubs (generated by the defeated male). This will cause the female to go into heat again, and then she becomes available for the reproduction of the young male's genes. The lioness tries hard to avoid the killing of her cubs, and when this finally happens she moans loudly for a couple of days, yet eventually she yields to her new inseminator. The documentary was delivered in the calm and focused tone of a scientist, and he did not call the killing of the cubs an act of injustice, but he referred to it as the typical example of "survival of the fittest" in nature.

While seeing these scenes, both the queen of hearts and the queen of clubs became active. I realized then how for the machine the sense of injustice could be felt as a legitimate experience. It seems that the queen of hearts and the queen of clubs are the organs that perceive when something "unjust" or "unkind" is done to one, to one's family and friends, to one's country, to life itself, or to humanity as a whole.

Humanity lives in what Gurdjieff called "the basement of the house", neglecting the higher floors where more beautiful and suitable rooms are designed for us. This means that most people experience their lives through the instinctive center alone, with all that it implies. Yet day after day we are quite surprised to see the laws that govern the instinctive center manifest in human beings.

The queens of centers draw us towards that which favors and improves life and well being, and they reject, disapprove, or draw us away from that which harms life and well being. Part of their function is to perceive, to attract, or to repulse.

However, as men number four we have to keep in mind that "to be in the queens" primarily means that our attention is controlled by the subject of interest and that we are likely identified with it. It does not matter whether the subject is the killing of the innocent, or the hopeless position of humanity as a whole, or simply one's partner treating one badly while in a bad mood. The point is that our attention is controlled from the outside.

Although for the queens the subject of identification in the moment is everything, our experience shows that once this subject disappears, they will find another one to fall for. I am sure that if any political party or tyrant, or any other circumstance in the universe becomes less of what we think it is, and more of what we would like it to be, the queen of hearts would find something else to disapprove.

Our work is to control the queens of centers. When we are in the king of hearts and king of diamonds we are closer to the realization that in our present state, we are far from understanding things as they are, so the question is, how do we get back to the kings more often?

Here is an aim that may help us move in that direction:

We can start from the creation of an attitude that will allow us to understand things as they are, firstly in ourselves. This attitude is based on acceptance of the fact that in the second state we perceive the world only partially, through a colored glass, but we cannot see it as it is. Later on, once this attitude has become permanent in us, we can start approaching the same subjects we were identified with from a more intelligent part. If we follow this line of action, next time we find ourselves worried about "unfair things that are happening in the universe" we can take that as a sign that we have fallen asleep.

One of the reasons why we cannot deal with ideas such as justice, good and evil, crime etc, is because we approach them with the wrong brain. We do not think properly, nor feel properly about them, and we often spend time considering about things that do not concern us.

Thus when pondering the significance of what we consider a crime or an injustice, we have to bring the subject down to our small scale. Both crime and injustice need men's thoughts and actions in order to manifest. All we can do is to make the aim not to be a vehicle through which this happens. And when we see it happening, we have to study the case impartially and figure out what in us allows crime or injustice to manifest.

For now, the only objective truth accessible to us is truth about ourselves, and that is what we have to focus on... Thus, Self Remembering and self-observation are our most urgent business.

There is no use talking to me, it is just the same as talking to you.

Robert Zimmerman

Self-Importance

The king of clubs is designed to keep the machine alive. It manipulates the energies of the four lower centers in order to ensure its biological and psychological survival. Biological survival is its proper field of action, for without the right work of this basic intelligence, life would most likely come to an end. Thus, the king of clubs makes sure it gets fed and sheltered; and it also perpetuates itself. It knows the place and the environment best for its survival, the friends and acquaintances that will ensure it. It will make the right alliances and divide those whose union is a threat, mark its territory and keep strangers and predators off its domain. It will respect the stronger ones and enforce the weaker ones' respect, etc...

As for its psychological survival, the king of clubs has to create an extra device: false personality.

Through false personality, the king of clubs allows the machine to live under the illusion of uniqueness. Thus, it surrounds itself with those people who support its self-importance and will take note of every slightly significant event in its life that might add to it: role, name, reputation, status within the tribe it happens to belong to. It does not matter whether the status is that of a misfit or a wise spiritual being, as long as the machine gets recognition from the tribe.

The lifetime of an individual human machine is insignificant on the scale of humanity (let alone organic life, the solar system and so on). But from the point of view of the machine itself, this insignificant span is all it has. Thus, all that this lifetime implies is of absolute importance for it.

Machines have to live, no matter how, from the beggar to the statesman, they all have to survive till their lives fully uncoil, and their existence must have a meaning within its insignificant span. Whether it is political, religious, or social or strictly personal it is all the same to organic life, all machines have to be kept alive.

From this point of view vanity might be seen as a key element of this cosmic device, designed to keep the machine asleep to the fact that the objective meaning of its existence does not take into consideration its worth as an individual.

Observing it as a device, there is no reason to identify with the machine's need to feel accepted, better, adequate, superior, different, cool, a victim, a misfit, a rebel or dissident. We can be present, shed light on this aspect of our mechanics and steadily follow Benjamin Franklin's suggestion to hide vanity from others as much as possible, for if we successfully diminish it, we will end up feeling proud of ourselves.

Tomorrow never knows.

R. Starkey

New Environment

Work on oneself when changing environment can be approached in two different ways; first from the point of view of the study of the machine, and second from the point of view of the study of Self Remembering as a new experience.

The first approach to this situation requires that we have the aim to create a deputy steward. That is, one "I" engaged in the observation and classification of the machine's different devices: centers and parts of centers, features, attitudes, groups of I's etc. The main quality of the deputy steward is that it functions from kings of centers, or controlled attention, and that its observations are recorded in relation to a greater whole: the study of the machine. It seems pertinent to associate the deputy steward with the quiet, neutral and focused voice of a scientist when he describes the behavior of some species of the animal kingdom.

During the first moments we spend in a new environment, for which the machine has not created a personality, our behavior comes from essence. This is a precious opportunity to verify the machine's essence; that is, its mechanical center of gravity and chief feature. For in such moments false personality has no clue as to how to behave. Provided we succeed in observing the machine in such circumstances, we can compare them to the first days spent at school, or at a new job, or even when we first joined the School.

On the other hand, there is another device to check while this is going on, namely, the king of clubs as it starts to tune the machine to its new social and psychological environment, so that it feels at home as soon as possible. This process is inevitable, just as at some point late at night, the king of clubs inevitably disconnects us from reality and puts us in the first state.

The deputy steward has to act quickly before the king of clubs turns the new experience into a familiar one. A further effort as we observe and study the machine is to detach our identity from what we observe; this is the task of the steward. It requires the same quality of attention but a greater will.

As regards the second and most important aspect of this circumstance, one of the first things Ouspensky mentions is that Self Remembering does occur in ordinary life (even from early childhood), without the actual effort to produce it by will. These moments of Self Remembering occur in new environments, in unexpected circumstances, while one is traveling, or in moments of extreme danger, when one "observes oneself from the outside". He does not mention the duration or depth of such moments, but simply acknowledges their appearance. I am sure every one of us, by making the effort to access his memory, will remember a few of these moments.

We may add that these moments of Self Remembering last very little, unless we make the continuous effort to make them last.   Still, simply knowing this already puts us in the position of studying them when they appear unexpectedly.   So we are lucky to know this when we are already or getting ready, to enter a new environment.

Carpe Diem!

God mingles not with man; all the intercourse and speech of God to man takes place through Eros.

Socrates

Fourth Way Religion

The following was written in response to a question regarding the meaning of the concept of "Fourth Way Religion", since our Teacher has recently used it in his meetings.

We may consider religion as a System of ideas or principles whose practice helps us connect to a higher world. Systems are created by or through men who have established a permanent connection with this higher (molecular or electronic) world while they still live in the cellular world. They translate their views from that world into a language suitable for those who are asleep to it.

Religion is essentially a practice, and our religion is called "The Work". Without the practice of the principles of the Work there is no religion, nor is there connection to Higher Forces, but rather self-deceit. The fulcrum of the Work is the effort to remember one's Self, since it is essential that we first become aware of the higher world within us.

Due to the different levels of being in men, religion is a relative term. Thus in our School, for example, (apart from those who have made a permanent connection with a higher world) there are different levels of men number four; and there are also men number one, two, and three who are in the process of becoming men number four.

Within our School, too, there are different levels of understanding of the term Religion.

Most of us practice the religion of men number four, which is a fluctuating situation. When we are in a higher state, we experience the religion of a man number five, yet when we are not making efforts our machines are simply men number one two or three. Therefore the words religion, system, school, higher forces are interpreted accordingly. When we are asleep the machine picks the most familiar aspects of the System and the School and creates its own imaginary religion, so to speak, which is basically an existential pacifier.

An objective approach to this subject is to verify where one stands from the point of view of religion, meaning whether one makes of the System as presented by Robert, the religion of a man number one, two, three or four.

When we think of the Fourth Way religion, we refer to the context of the different ways of attaining self awareness and awareness of Higher Forces: namely the way of the fakir, the way of the monk, and the way of the yogi.

The Fourth Way is based on verification, that is, on direct knowledge of things as they are. Yet it also includes some aspects that we cannot verify at the moment, so we have to approach them from a philosophical or theoretical point of view alone. No need to make a dogma of things we cannot verify, such as the Celestial City of Paradise, the Absolute, or the theory of eternal life.

Machines tend to embrace different explanations of subjects that are difficult, if not impossible to verify in the second state, depending on their type and center of gravity: some people prefer Rodney Collin; some prefer Robert, Plotinus, Plato or the Koran: It is useful to keep this in mind as a point of reference.

Given the fact that we are trapped within the laws that govern the cellular world we can only verify so much, and we are aware of the great effort and concentration it takes to do so. What we can verify this very moment is that through the effort to sustain and divide attention, we actually enter the molecular world, which is the primary aim of every religion.

We are to judge with reverence, and with greater acknowledgment of our own infirmity.

Montaigne

Judgment I's

One of the things we have discovered about judgment I's is that every machine has a limited repertoire, that is, it judges specific manifestations in a number of machines, not all manifestations in all machines. Thus, judgment I's can be very useful for the study of our own mechanics. We can observe them, for example, from the point of view of the study of centers and parts of centers, or body type and chief feature, or false personality.

While working with judgment I's it is necessary to keep in mind the principle of the Work that one is not what one observes, but one is the observer (in this case the deputy steward. Thus, when working with these I's we are above all creating or reinforcing an "I" or group of I's engaged in the study of the machine in a totally detached and neutral way.

Paradoxically we have to refrain from judging judgment I's; just observe them and record them, because they are false personality in disguise.

A useful way to study judgment I's is to take one person at a time ad work with him or her for a while.

It can be one's boss, another student, one's partner, the Teacher, one's center director, a friend. Then observe and record –write down if necessary- all the I's (both positive and negative) the machine produces in relation to the chosen person. Then try to figure out what center, what feature or combination of features they could come from. If in doubt ask other students' opinions about the origin of each manifestation and try to verify what they say. This way the attention is withdrawn from the person and becomes focused on our own machine, which is our real subject of study.

If we practice this long enough we discover an interesting characteristic of our present state. Namely, while we remain disconnected from higher centers, our perception of others depends on the device or devices at work at a given moment. That is why it is important to take one person at a time and record all the I's the machine produces in relation to them. Sometimes we perceive one person from the point of view of the queen of hearts, or the king of clubs, other times from the moving or the intellectual center; yet other times from our chief feature, sex center, programming etc…

When we speak of judgment I's we usually refer to negative, extreme opinions about others, in which case we might be referring to the negative half of the queen of hearts. This in turn, means we have to find ways to raise our level of attention in the emotional center in that moment.

In this area it is especially useful to let our friends

know that we are working on judgment I's, so that we have their help, plus we may turn false personality's accomplices for judgment into allies of our work.

Never confuse motion with action.

B. Franklin

What is Momentum?

Momentum can be seen as the mechanical force an action takes after we make the initial effort to perform it. Our experience shows that jacks and queens of centers are the carriers of such force; kings of centers stand for continuous effort to control attention.

Self-Remembering requires an effort every three seconds, therefore the idea of momentum does not apply here.

In the beginning, most of us cannot be in the kings for long, nor remember ourselves at will. In order to raise our attention and reach a higher state we have to use indirect methods, such as putting the machine in situations out of patterns, or shocking the lower centers. Such methods force us to be in the kings of centers and from there we can make the effort to experience our Self.

When we break the machine's momentum by shocking the lower centers, we see energy is released and our level of attention increases for a few seconds or minutes. When shocking lower centers it is necessary to have the aim to make further efforts to sustain attention: in other words, *momentum can only be stopped by continuous effort.*

The initial effort is to be in kings of centers while the energy of the shock circulates within the machine. Even if we cannot divide our attention, we can still sustain the effort to remain attentive and work from there. The tendency of the machine is to let go completely and go back to sleep for days or weeks. That is, when we stop making efforts the energy released by the shock goes into negative emotions or into imagination, we fall back in the jacks of centers; back into mechanical momentum

The external shocks we create in order to break the machine's momentum do not necessarily have to be blunt, violent, or negative. They can be as subtle as opening the door and letting the wind blow into the room, or shifting to a slightly uncomfortable position as we sit. The point is to learn how to use the energy released by the shock, to make an effort and control our attention.

Keep the experience in mind.

Being able to stop momentum is only the initial effort. When we learn to further sustain attention, on the one hand we meet face to face the tremendous mechanical force that keeps us asleep, and on the other hand, we experience our infant Self, still dim, in so much need of our efforts.

Mystical knowledge proceeds not from wit, but from experience; it is not invented but proved, not read but received.

Miguel de Molinos

Interpreting B Influence

This letter was written in response to a question about the ability of men number four to interpret one of Christ's Parables.[6]

We all agree that the Parables are B influence. There is no direct connection between us and the source of such information, thus their precise meaning is, so to speak, temporarily locked away for us, just as Beelzebub's Tales is. Additionally, there are so many versions of the Gospels that have gone through Christ only know how many translations and interpretations throughout the centuries. So what chances does a man number four have to understand their deepest meaning? While in the second state, one can at best offer one's subjective interpretations. And we will probably get as many as the amount of students who will participate in the discussion.

Christ's teaching was delivered in a specific language and it was primarily meant for his inner circle. In our School we too have a specific language (described at the prospective student meetings), which has proven to be clear and efficient. It is as simple as

6 The letter was written five years before Robert focused his teaching on esoteric keys from The Bible, the Koran, Sufi, Mesoamerican and Egyptian literature.

True, False, Higher, Lower, A, B, C and 1,2,3,4,5,6,7. False personality sometimes distracts us by trying to find translations from a dead language into the living language of our System.

Now if we deeply wish to "live" the questions that arise from our B influence readings, we have to experience directly, through self-observation and Self Remembering, the key elements written on the texts we read. Thus look for and study terms, such as in the case of the "Parable of the Weeds" for example, "corn", "seed", "enemy", "weed" and so on, see what devices or mechanics they reflect. Additionally, taking into consideration the historical context within which they were created, try to find out what value was given to these terms. If you think it is useful translate them into terms of the System.

In this case we will be trying to translate reality as we experience it when we are in a higher state, into a language suitable for lower centers. Is it not what Robert does when he quotes Christ, Ouspensky, Berenson, the Greeks, Leonardo, and even sometimes folk singers of our times?

When that which is perfect is come then that which is in part shall be done away.

Cristina Rossetti

Types

Every machine is the result of the combined work of all seven glands and all three aspects of the nervous System. The effect of glands on personality is what we call "features". One gland produces more than one feature or psychological attribute, depending on the influences (both internal and external) to which it responds in the moment. A solar-lunar machine for example, can manifest through willfulness or it can be cold blooded, or cautious, or experience fear or lunatic I's. If we add to it all features possible in a Solar, plus all features programmed by its social environment, our study gets more and more complex.

When we study types, we do so from the point of view of "the play of features", that is, how features influence and interact with each other, and it might be better to pin our study down to one feature at a time.

Study of other people's mechanics helps us realize that the human body is a machine that functions according to specific laws. Luckily, self-observation brings us to a deeper understanding of these laws. The issue is no longer "man is a sleeping machine" but that Rolando is a sleeping machine. Yet we must never forget that self-observation is one part of the machine observing other parts. Because when we forget it, we feel we are these machines, thus sometimes we experience the emotions of being funny, or awkward; we get terrified or worse.

Rodney Collin observes that we can only recognize and classify types from a higher state, that is, when we are not subject to our own type or feature. *Then we are Divine Presence witnessing mechanical laws.* Now when we remain at the level of the machine; we feel we are mechanical, we get scared or feel funny, or laugh about ourselves. Sometimes we even bring ourselves to the verge of an emotional or mental breakdown. Yet our true identity is in the third state and we realize the machine in its temporary existence. We simply understand it in silence.

Self-remembering is the effort to separate our identity from the machine (the activity of the glands and the nervous system.) With Self-remembering the "feeling" is more like "I am in this machine that sees the world through a colored filter. This body type or set of features stands between me and reality."

The question then is "How can I be awake more often".

Once we verify we are trapped in machines, we understand that the knowledge of types and features is a tool that allows us to escape the influence of these machines.

Another practical use of this tool is coexistence in conformity with other types, since in our School we are working together towards a common higher aim. By getting to know our own type and how it reacts to other types, we may act more intentionally when dealing with people.

Eventually each of us will have to become aware of their own type, of their talent and weakness, in order to understand their role in serving this higher aim. This implies the study and control of one's own feature in the moment. It also requires the realization that one is not the type, nor the feature. One is the Self being born invisibly, one effort at a time, in the service of Higher Forces.

For now we see through a glass, darkly.

Paul

Features

A feature can be seen as the consequence of the release in the organism of a substance with definite characteristics called a *hormone*. It is the release of this substance that produces in the machine the subjective experiences of fear, haste or boredom; or the need of controlling the environment, or the wish to take care of others. Features are thus chemistry at work set in motion by external circumstances and shocks, such as conscious influence, accidents, people, and planets. When a hormone is released, in a fraction of a second the whole physical sensation of the machine gets modified. The machine's mood changes, its emotions shift accordingly, and later on the slowest of the brains follows up producing notions that will support the way the machine relates to the world.

For a number of us traveling by plane, for example, take-off and landing are circumstances that set our adrenals to work. Yet while some types experience such intense molecular activity only in this specific instance, the adrenal type is meant to experience it on a regular basis, even in cases when there is no potential danger.

This means that in every machine there is a feature or gland more active than the others: this is the machine's chief feature in essence. If we were in essence, we would always respond from this feature, but there is also a chief feature in personality, which for a while prevents a man number four from being aware of his chief feature in essence.

Chief feature in false personality can be very useful because, given the fact that it is possible to carefully dismantle it and eliminate it, during this process we create tools and learn techniques that we can use later on in order to control chief feature in essence. Just as our whole physiognomy cannot be modified, our chief feature in essence cannot be eliminated; it can only be hidden when needed. This way its effects never reach the outside world.

Chief feature in personality has been programmed artificially. Take for example machines with passive features, whose mother or father's active features constantly trained or forced them to behave in a way opposite to their essence. In such machines, the glands that produce active features are set to work by mechanical means such as repetition, threats, tricks or treats, abuse, punishment, reward.

The fact that it is possible to set a given gland to work by artificial means proves it is possible to control features through intentional attitudes and aims. In case the feature is in personality, it is meant to disappear and give way to essence, in case it is in essence, we can turn it into our major skill in our Work. Power feature for example, wants to control and manipulate others, yet when directed towards our own machine, can be very useful to achieve self-control.

Finally, every circumstance requires a specific line of action or inaction, yet features respond the same way all of the time. Sometimes the moment requires that we wait or stay aloof, sometimes it requires that we act quickly, sometimes that we ponder, so the point is to be present to the needs of the moment and act as we are required. At times this implies we have to control our features because their participation would be more of an intrusion or an obstacle, yet other times their activity may prove a useful contribution.

Man's worst deceits are his own opinions.

Leonardo Da Vinci

Play of Features[7]

For a long time our efforts in first line are connected primarily to the development of a deputy steward, which implies that our aim is the study of the System and of our own mechanics from the point of view of the System. Study of other people's mechanics is not our priority, yet we pursue it in connection to the study of our own mechanics and mechanicality in general.

When we observe features in others, we may want to study them from the point of view of what we call in the Work a "play of features", so that we may study our own mechanics simultaneously with the study of other people's. When for a few seconds we withdraw our attention from other people's mechanics and direct it toward our own, we realize that in our sleep, a feature in us is reacting to a feature in them. We have to ask ourselves, What is this feature?

However, there is a risk that the queen of hearts takes over and pretends to be the "Observing I"; thus we find ourselves "observing" and talking almost exclusively about other machines' features. Additionally, the king of clubs (the part of the machine that is always alert) will not allow us to direct attention towards ourselves,

7 We refer to *a play of features* as the way features react and relate to each other.

or study and work on ourselves.

The queen of hearts is a very good instrument of perception in the moment: it helps us see things about others and about ourselves directly; but it has to be at the service of our deputy steward, otherwise it works at the service of the king of clubs.

Therefore we need to make it a special aim to observe and study our own mechanics and the way they interact with other people's, and keep always in mind "we are not what we observe, we are the observers".

Addendum:

The following note was later added to the text in response to a student's request to explain the phrase "...*The queen of hearts has to be at the service of our deputy steward, otherwise it works at the service of the king of clubs...*"

The king of clubs has one aim: the survival of the machine, both biological and psychological. In order to ensure the psychological survival of the machine it creates and supports an imaginary picture.

In order to verify this, try dividing your attention when someone offers you a photograph that affects the machine's imaginary picture. You will see that the king of clubs marks that other person.

The queen of hearts enters here, since it is the device

in the machine which can provide in the moment accurate observations about other people's strengths and weaknesses: thus it will become active every time the other person shows up in your environment. Since in this case it is at the service of the king of clubs, it will look for mechanics in the other person in order to put them down, or up, depending on the nature of the machine's imaginary picture of the other person.

The aim of the deputy steward is the study of the System and one's own machine from the point of view of waking up and trying to remain awake.

The study of other people's mechanics is valid inasmuch as it helps us understand a specific device we happen to be studying in us.

Say we are studying the feature of vanity. We have to learn to recognize it every time it manifests in a machine. Sometimes we will see it manifesting in our own machine, sometimes we will see it manifesting in our partner's, or our center director's, or a work mate. But since the subject of our study is vanity itself, our deputy steward will not be concerned with judging the vehicle through which it manifests the moment we recognize it.

When we are in the level of attention we call the deputy steward we understand the reason why we are making observations of certain mechanics. Yet when we fall asleep, the king of clubs can easily make use of the very same precious observations for its own private agenda.

Always bear in mind that your own resolution to succeed is more important than any other one thing.

Abraham Lincoln

School Exercises

At this stage we cannot access the third state at will, all we can do is make the aim to increase the frequency of moments when we make efforts to reach it, therefore increase our chances of remembering.

Sometimes Robert encourages us to approach Self Remembering indirectly: through direct work on functions. For example, he gives us exercises like, to taste our food, to hear the sounds around us, to feel our feet on the ground, to be intentional with our movements. These exercises are all related to the effort to remember one's Self through the development of attention in the moving instinctive center. Whereas exercises like to avoid gossip, not express negativity, not to judge, to take in fine impressions, consider externally, are all related to the effort to remember one's Self through the development of attention in the emotional center. Then to stop thoughts, study the System or not to think in opposites, refers to the effort to remember one's Self through the development of attention in the intellectual center.

Exercises require will: the will to be present. Without presence, exercises are carried out by the king of clubs. The king of clubs has a special interest in exercises. Because they represent, in the full sense of the term, the external form of a School. And it knows that by attaching to them as the ultimate aim, it will keep the steward in the world of make-believe.

C Influence is only possible through the organization of a School, though this might have many meanings as yet unrecognized by us.

R. Collin

Moving away from B influence

According to Rodney Collin, B influence consists of crystallized traces of C Influence. Robert points out that to pursue influence B is a form of sleep which creates the illusion of pursuing awakening. Initially B influence was C Influence, since it was designed by a conscious teacher for his closer disciples, or inner circle, with the aim to work directly on each student according to his type and level of being. Each student receives the right information in order to work on himself efficiently. The moment this same information is made available outside the inner circle it starts to become less and less personal, until it finally becomes a doctrine, a religious ritual, a spiritual text, a work of art and so on.

Ouspensky's "In Search of the miraculous" Robert's "Self Remembering" or Girard's "Creating a Soul" are B influence. They come from a conscious origin, but their effect sooner or later becomes mechanical. Some of us have verified that for example, when Robert speaks at a dinner table, he addresses directly the people present there. Sometimes he gives specific information to a student. Other times he asks someone to write down a phrase he delivered and turn it into a Daily Card, thus choosing to share the information outside of the context wherein it originated[8].

Now Daily Cards travel around the School and every time they reach us when we are in lower parts of centers, they often give rise to speculation, polemics, or become superstition or blind religion. Thus we verify how the influence of a conscious being can become mechanical within his School. If we consider this influence further away from the inner circle, (Robert's book can be found in B influence bookstores) we have no idea of who will ever purchase or read this book, what they will make of it, or whether it will ever reach a person with a magnetic center.

We may remember that when B influence reached us, it fed our magnetic center. But once we arrived to the School, we started to receive more specific information related to each of us as an individual: that is, we started to receive C Influence.

In right order, we move away from B influence as we begin to recognize and work with C Influence. In order to make this possible, our magnetic center must yield to the creation of a deputy steward. Indeed some aspects of the magnetic center can be useful for the creation of the deputy steward, but most have to be discarded.

---

8 The article was written long before Robert decided to have some of his teaching events video recorded.

Sometimes students create a magnetic center based on their king of clubs, therefore they tend to become interested and even caught up in some forms of B influence, because these satisfy lower centers. The king of clubs prefers B influence to C Influence since the latter guarantees no gratification on the level of the machine.

In other cases, even within a conscious school, our king of clubs still tends to diminish C Influence, bringing it down to the level of B influence, or even A influence. In our School it tends to diminish Robert's tasks and exercises, sometimes through active resistance, but also making dogmas or absolute laws out of them.

Here are some observations from students, gathered during a meeting at the Venice center, regarding how the king of clubs diminishes higher influences.

- Information about Types becomes influence B when we do not use it as a tool for self-observation and work on chief feature. The queen of hearts uses it for small talk and for judgment.
- Laziness does not like to verify information coming from the Teacher; it is satisfied with taking it as an absolute truth without trying to verify it.
- The machine tends to project the image of its father, or of some past or present spiritual leader into our Teacher.

- In other cases Influence C is diminished to the level of influence A, for example when one asks the Teacher whether one should marry or change jobs. In fact our Teacher says that some students want to use him as their janitor.

Through Self Remembering we prevent Influence C from becoming mechanical in us as we receive it.

Influence B has played an important role in our lives, it has helped us create a magnetic center, and more importantly, it has helped us find Influence C. It was said before that some aspects of the magnetic center could be useful for the creation of the deputy steward; however some of its remnants sooner rather than later have to be eliminated:

- Curiosity about different ways and Teachers.
- Faith without effort.
- Desire to find the meaning of life on the level of the machine.
- Wish and hope for peace on earth.
- Psychological well being.
- Superstition.

All of these and more remnants of our magnetic center can become interested in B influence. Whoever has verified C Influence must disallow these manifestations, for they are a form of regression. Real possibilities of awakening depend on our connection with C Influence. B influence is safer for the machine because it does not imply any serious work on oneself. Every time we deal with this influence, in reality we deal with the remnants of our magnetic center, or with laziness: the king of clubs trying to escape real work.

Ouspensky tells us that the magnetic center has to be created in the king of hearts: the emotional intelligence in the machine, otherwise we will fail in our attempts to awaken. Only when we are in the king of hearts can we discriminate between C influence and B influence. It is also from this level of attention that we can make organized efforts to reach higher centers. Another definition we give to the king of hearts is "The door towards higher centers".

A question that often arises is: Does our connection with C Influence depend on them alone, or is there anything we can do in order to remain connected to them?

Connection with C Influence requires an effort from both sides; otherwise the situation is nothing more than unrequited love. Though often we cannot foresee when or how we will receive their direct influence, we can still make efforts on our side; make ourselves ready.

In order to receive and understand their messages, shocks and precise instructions, it is necessary to keep in mind the nature and reason of our relationship with C Influence; namely, they are helping us in our aim to escape the prison of the machine. Thus, we have to accumulate, through Self Remembering and self-observation, enough material related to our own machine's tendencies. Self Remembering helps us see the weakness that keeps us asleep in the moment. It is then that we are in the position to receive influence coming from a conscious source without wasting it.

Each student's machine is a role that implies a definite task, and definite weaknesses to overcome. C Influence works in the present to create the right conditions for each individual soul to perform his task, overcome his weakness.

It is necessary that we verify our sleep over and over. It is necessary that we deeply wish to awaken; otherwise when Influence C tries to wake us up we will resent it. On the other hand, it is obvious that when we sleep, whether we are dreaming sweet or sour dreams about Robert, the School or the Higher Forces, we are disconnected from them.

Refine the sexual energy upward.

Lao Tzu

Sex and Feminine Dominance

It is difficult to observe and talk about the most elusive parts of the machine, whose combination represents probably the major obstacle to awakening. On the one hand we are dealing with the brain that keeps us connected to feminine dominance, the intelligence that rules every machine: the king of clubs. On the other hand we have the sex center, the brain we cannot study directly unless we are present; the brain whose work uses up the very substance our soul is made of.

Initially it is better to keep our study on a clinical level, therefore to refrain from thinking, "I feel attracted", "I want", "I like", but instead think in terms of "the king of clubs" or "the sex center". When we attended the prospective student meetings we learned how the king of clubs works, not how certain kings of clubs work, or how the sex center works, not how some sex centers work... etc. The law is one and the same; we are simply studying the variety of its manifestations.

We have to keep in mind that the king of clubs prefers not to touch the subject of sex, unless in private conversations, gossip or small talk. Most times it will not allow other parts of the machine to access that information. This proves that the machine's sense of identity is attached to both of these brains, in some cases guarded by the negative emotion of fear.

I will first share some observations in relation to the sex center and then some related to the king of clubs and its domain: feminine dominance.

As regards the sex center, it is possible to verify how the machine's sense of identity gets attached to its functioning when we experience a strong reciprocal attraction. The machine feels that another machine it feels attracted to is special and unique, and at the same moment the other machine makes ours feel special and unique. In right order, this feeling of uniqueness touches essence, not false personality. The notion, "the love of one's life" is related to an event of this kind. Nothing but "the other" matters to me, nothing but "I" matter to the other. Both machines are ready to do anything in order to be together. On the level of the machine, this is probably the highest experience in life. Anyone on earth is meant to have it, and when it is over, some machines never recover from having lost the "love of their lives". Tolstoy's novel Anna Karenina is a good example in literature, but I am sure every one of us has tasted it to some extent, at least once.

There is, however, a poor substitute to this event; that is when false personality takes over and tries to actively attract other people's attention. False personality makes the machine feel special because it is able to attract the attention of more than one member of the opposite sex, regardless of our commitments, or the commitments of the people involved. In this case, most of the Soul's patrimony is spent on the idle sport of seduction. According to my observations, the Self cannot be created when we are engaged in such activity, but what actually happens is that we are strengthening the king of clubs, while throwing away the substance the soul is made of. Gurdjieff would call this "masturbation" which basically means, something that stands for the "real thing".

Every time one experiences a strong mechanical attraction either when one is already in a relationship or when one feels it toward someone who is already in a relationship, it is not an easy situation to work with. While Tolstoy's "Anna Karenina" shows how this mechanical event develops effortlessly into a descending octave, Goethe's "Elective Affinities" presents us with both, the descending and the ascending octave. Although in some cases a strong attraction may cause our king of clubs to question the validity of our relationship, what must rule our relationship with others is the king of hearts (emotional intelligence) for only that part in us can consider them on the same level as we wish to be considered.

Again, many of us might have had similar experiences in this area, but the king of clubs will not let us think about it, it is very careful not to deal with its own sexual inclinations... it would rather "study" or focus on other people's.

The second aspect of the subject is feminine dominance:

We know the sex center does not have a mechanical negative part. In order to control its manifestations an artificial negative part has to be developed. This negative part comes from the education, or from the manipulation of the four lower centers. Every society produces its own form of feminine dominance in order to control sexual behavior.

Marriage is one of those forms, the Harem another one, there are some societies that allow a man to have only as many wives as he may properly support etc. In the past, when Matriarchal societies were dominant, there was no need for the form of marriage. The line of inheritance was on the female side; therefore the male did not have relevance as a father nor as a provider as we understand it nowadays. A woman could have kids from as many males as she found fit, and could dispose of partners once their job was done. As I understand now, forms such as Harem and Marriage were initially instituted in order to ensure the line of inheritance on the male's side.

Our School thrives within a multiethnic society still in the process of creation; and we often run into each other's old form of feminine dominance. Also, as time goes by, the king of clubs creates a new form of feminine dominance based on a mixture of its understanding of its old form, and the form of the School. It does it through rules of the School such as the sex exercise[9],

9 The sex exercise required students to refrain from sex outside of marriage. It has now been withdrawn.

marriage, betrothal, friendship, the Work and other labels. When it prefers to feel safe within its social group, it punctually follows the rules, when it feels self confident and strong enough to stand on its own, it does not need to.

We have to study the specific kind of feminine dominance our king of clubs is attached to, which is different for every machine, and then we have to find our way out of it, without necessarily changing anything outside of ourselves.

So far in our society Robert has chosen to keep the form of marriage and one of our tasks is to find ways to realize its highest possibilities. In order to accomplish this, we need to constantly remember that partners are individuals who are in the process of becoming real women and real men; thus they have to be dealt with much care and understanding, as if they were buds or infants. Then marriage becomes a ground where men number four can support each other's development. Apart from the inevitable mechanical aspects of marriage, we have to introduce a conscious aspect to it, based on the Work; that is external consideration. External consideration implies that we have to get acquainted with our partner's strengths, weaknesses, tastes, inclinations, hopes, fears so that we do not act thoughtlessly in their regard. Additionally, in the School, we see our partner primarily as someone who is trying to awaken, and who knows we are trying to awaken. Thus, his or her awakening must be a priority above all other common interests.

It is also useful to study, and not to buffer the mechanical aspects of a marriage: for example harmonious physical sex, interests such as status, money, play of features, family, fear of the unknown, inertia, mechanical goodness, age, comfort. When we recognize these forces that may keep our marriages working on a mechanical level, we do not necessarily have to give way to disillusion and, as we sometimes do, shift partners. But we can build a higher relationship with our partner, above and beyond mechanical interests that may bind us together.

We all have an instinctive center, and we know it sees its partner in terms of its own advantage, yet that does not necessarily prevent our Self from being present to him/her as a spiritual being, as an individual who joined the School with the understanding that below the thin layer of ordinary life may grow, invisible, a higher form of existence.

Every day we should appreciate a work of art, read a poem, and where possible, say a few sensible words.

Goethe

Educating Essence

The education of essence requires that we work simultaneously on several areas. First we have to determine our machine's essence: body type, chief feature, center of gravity, and alchemy. In order to attain this we have to discover the origin of every manifestation in our machine, with the aim of discriminating between that which is truly our own and that which comes from education, imitation, domestication, or simple reaction to the outside world. Also it is important to become aware of the age at which our essence's development stopped.

The second area of work in this area is the development of true personality, for only when we are in true personality can we undertake the education of essence. We also have to remember that the development of true personality runs parallel with the undoing of false personality, or imaginary picture. This means on the one hand, to give up the wrong attitudes that create our imaginary picture, and on the other hand the intentional creation of new attitudes based on the principles given to us by our Teacher, the School and conscious beings of the past.

In the beginning we try to focus on weeding false personality from the flower of essence. Yet essence is not always a flower but a tiny bud, therefore we have to be very careful when weeding. Some of us, whose imaginary picture was that of "a millenary oak", were quite surprised to find out we were simply tiny buds. This is one of the reasons why it is important that the dismantlement of false personality runs parallel with the development of true personality.

Essence must not be left without protection.

When we begin to be present to our own essence we may agree with Girard's statement when he says "... experience of essence is often accompanied by a sense of child-like freedom and light heartedness." Gurdjieff is rather tough on his description when he says, *"As a rule a man's essence is primitive, savage and childish, or simply stupid."*

Some aspects of our essence remained undeveloped and we have to learn to face this truth without judgment. We may verify this when we observe the different kinds of friction we give to other people. Sometimes it is our false personality that gives friction to others. That is, although we behave like adults, we are quite unpleasant to them. Yet other times, manifestations from our undeveloped essence give friction to other people, meaning our behavior is below the level of maturity expected from us.

We know we need to be in essence if we want to

become conscious; yet it has been pointed out that essence has to be developed and educated beyond its child-like state. One of the first things we see when we experience essence is that it is not interested in Self Remembering, nor in working beyond its level of being. Thus, work on oneself must begin from true personality, which is rooted in the development of the king of hearts.

Robert indicates three ways of nourishing essence: beauty, kindness and suffering.

Beauty
True personality selects the right influences, the right friendships and relations that will help essence become nobler. Also true personality understands the need to expose essence to higher impressions such as music, painting, poetry, etc. And what is more important, it understands the need to teach essence to create higher impressions (thoughts, emotions, actions) for others. Here is where Goethe's words remind us of that necessity. *"Every day we should ...where possible, say a few sensible words"*.

Kindness
On the one hand, kindness means to be kind towards one's own essence (provided one knows its true nature and sensibility) yet it also means to teach one's essence to be kind towards other people. The tools to educate essence in this respect are simple: not to express negativity, not to judge, consider other people as you would like them to consider you. To expect kindness

from other people towards us is not a work idea, but a limitation of essence.

Suffering

When we work with pushing essence beyond its level of being, we are ready to put it in circumstances where it will have to make efforts, regardless of its wants and inclinations. When we work on features and weaknesses in personality they eventually disappear. It is not the same when we work on features and weaknesses in essence; for given the fact that they are part of the infrastructure of the machine, they are meant to stay with us throughout this lifetime. Thus when we think of educating essence we need to calculate the mechanical resistance it will pose, and the suffering it will imply to push it beyond this limitation. For example a student with a machine centered in the queen of hearts will always have a hard time being patient. A mercurial will always have a hard time following the School exercises and Robert's indications etc.

Although we receive the System through true personality, it is through essence that we have to make efforts to turn it into being. Otherwise our efforts will simple be the imitation the external form of the School, or the repetition of the work ideas without real understanding.

Judge by the truth; the truth is in the present.

Ibn Arabi

Getting to know others

Getting to know other people requires that we make the effort to remember ourselves in relation to them. We know we have I's about others which come from lower parts of centers, but we try not to identify with them. Our true identity is in Self Remembering, that is, in the direct experience of that which is divine within us. Every time we relate to others from the higher in ourselves, we are in a better position to experience the higher in them, for it is there where they too search for their own identity.

As long as our conscience remains trapped in lower parts of centers, we will not be able to recognize the higher in others. Lower parts are designed to see only what interests them. For example, the queen of clubs may only see others in terms of how they spoil or support the machine's comfort. False personality in turn, may only see others in terms of those who acknowledge and support it and those who don't.

Work in this area requires that we constantly return to higher parts in us. In other words control attention by will, both in the emotional and in the intellectual center as we try to be present to people. According to Robert, the king of hearts has a mechanism that can learn to appreciate others without identification. He is an example of this, since he makes every one of his students feel special every time he meets them.

We can verify that we are developing the king of hearts when we see ourselves trying to understand others, instead of judging them according to the way false personality thinks they should behave, or what area they should work on in order to accept them.

Trying to understand others means seeing them from the point of view of their evolution.

It is a law that the lower cannot see the higher, yet the higher can shed light on the lower... in silence.

In my past life I had tried everything, even had worn reminding factors of all kinds on my person.

Gurdjieff

Rock Music

At some point, the Teacher gave us the exercise to refrain from listening to Rock music, as it was not meant to be a part of the form of the School. Some of us had a hard time giving up this type of music. The following text was written in response to a question about how to find practical ways to work with this exercise.[10]

A request or an exercise coming from the Teacher is primarily an opportunity to develop will. At the same time we can study the way our machine reacts to it. That alone will give us enough material to work with. Yet some of us may wish to explore where rock music stands within the context of the whole spectrum of music.

In this respect I would like to share an experiment I made with a couple of other students, which has shed light on the essence of Rock music. Like any other experiment, this required the aim and effort to divide attention plus the aim to observe the lower functions.

We gathered a few CD's with different music and turned on the stereo.

---

10 This is exercise has now been rescinded.

The different pieces were, amongst others:

> Tina Turner's "Steamy Widows"
> Bruce Springsteen's "Hungry heart"
> Dave Brubeck's "Take Five"
> Puccni's "Mi chiamano Mimi" from "La Boheme"
> A movement from Vivaldi's "L'Estro Armonico"
> A segment from Bach's "Goldberg Variations"
> A cradlesong named "Oh my little boy..."

I do not wish to go into detail as to which piece produced what reaction in our machines. I will just mention that different pieces evoked different centers and parts of centers. Sometimes we found ourselves merrily tapping our feet on the floor. Sometimes a smile grew on our faces. Yet some other times, given the fact that the music we were listening to required the effort to sustain attention, our machines tended to drift into imagination. Some music addressed the intellectual parts of centers, some the emotional, some the moving- instinctive parts. Some pumped sex energy into the instinctive center. Some required effort to listen, some did not.

Anyone interested in figuring out this aspect of the essence of Rock music or any other music may wish to try this exercise.

Another way to deepen our understanding in relation to Rock music as a form of expression is to unload from the Internet the following tunes. Read through the lines and try to understand the message they carry in them:

> Patty Smith's "Space Monkey"
> Tina Turner's "Steamy Windows"
> Rod Stewart's "I was only joking"
> Pink Floyd's "Wish you were here"
> Frank Zappa's "Jewish Princess"
> Kinks' "Celluloid Heroes"
> Beatles' "Tomorrow never knows"
> Lou Reed's "Heroine"
> Rolling Stones' "Some Girls"
> Bob Dylan's "Forever Young"

If you are not a native English speaker it is essential that you translate them, or have them translated into your own language so that you can understand what these songs do talk about. Verify whether or not they support your aims.

Some of us find it hard to give up listening to Rock music because some of its main writers, who at the time had a magnetic center, or seemed to have one, fed our own. But we keep in mind that for us, "the answer is not blowing in the wind anymore".

In relation to the evolution of the spirit, Pilate is a stop. For a man of real inner development there can be no "washing of hands".

Ouspensky

Photographs as Shocks to Conscience

This article is the result of a series of notes written after a meeting on conscience. The meeting was introduced with an interpretation of the role of Judas in Christ's passion play.

Interpretations of the role of Judas vary depending on the people who ponder it. Ouspensky, for example, refers to Judas as a little man who found himself in the wrong place; an ordinary man who understood nothing of what Christ taught to his disciples. Ouspensky said that Judas' psychology is quite humane. It is the psychology of he who denigrates what he does not understand. Ouspensky does not even consider Judas a role but a stimulus-response machine. Rodney Collin instead, describes Judas as an example of how one can consciously play an apparently abominable role in such a way that one can make oneself ready for "*the next one*". He implies that Judas' role was necessary for the soul playing it. Gurdjieff speaks of Judas more or less in the same terms, since he assumes that Christ knew he was meant to die, it had already been decided. His disciples knew it too, and each of them knew the role he had to play[11]. Robert, in turn, said that the biggest crime of humanity was when Judas betrayed Christ with a kiss. There is also the traditional interpretation of Judas' role the petty egoistical Jew who does not hesitate to sell Christ for thirty silver coins.

A student suggested that in his last supper, Leonardo Da Vinci portrayed in the face of Judas the contradictory emotions he was experiencing as Christ said, "*One of you who ate with me shall betray me[12]*". According to this interpretation, at that moment Judas experienced a flash of conscience. He knew exactly what he was doing, he understood it was a mistake to sell his Teacher, and he acted knowingly in the wrong direction. Curiously enough, Ouspensky uses Pilate and not Judas as an example to illustrate this psychological failure. He says that Pilate saw and understood the truth perfectly. But political or personal interests forced him to betray the truth and "*wash his hands*".

As students in a conscious school, we cannot afford any "washing of hands" or betrayal of the truth. And because one of our first aims is to know the truth about ourselves, we have to become aware of, and learn to separate from, the weakness that compels us to "wash our hands"; the feature that is ready to "sell our conscience for thirty pieces of silver".

11 This article was written before the publishing of the *Gospel of Judas*

12 Leonardo's "Last Supper" in Santa Maria delle Grazie (Milan) represents this moment in Christ's Passion play.

Conscience is difficult to bear because it implies awareness of the truth about us as individuals. In one split second we become aware of whom we are as opposed to who we dream we are, and what we are supposed to be doing as opposed to what we imagine to be doing. If we were coherent with what we think, say and do, the manifestation of our conscience would be a blessing. Yet we have verified that more than often we think one thing, say something else and go ahead and do something completely different. Thus, only a few are interested in the experience of conscience, for it seems more like a curse.

"... Because everyone has within him thousands of contradictory feelings, which vary from a deeply hidden realization of his own nothingness and fears of all kinds, to the most stupid kind of self conceit, self confidence, self satisfaction and self praise, to feel all this together would not only be painful but literally unbearable."
Gurdjieff

The tool of photographing one another is one way to get everyone familiar with the taste of conscience, and therefore a way to learn to bear the truth about ourselves.

Photographs come from all levels of attention, centers of gravity, body types etc. But what interests us is that they serve as shocks that unveil those aspects of our mechanics that our features manage to hide from us. Thus, we have to make a permanent aim to try to neutrally verify every photograph or observation we are offered. Sometimes we will actually verify that the photograph is incorrect, and that will be the end of it. Yet when we verify that the photograph is right, we can consider ourselves lucky, and be grateful towards the person who has brought us nearer to the truth.

Ideally, any reaction from other people that reaches our field of awareness should be an alarm clock that spurs us to figure out what in us made them react a certain way. Say, for example, you turn up the light in the room where a meeting is about to take place without asking anybody's opinion. Then one student will photograph power feature in you, another one will photograph your instinctive center taking space, yet a third one will simply thank you for doing it. There you have three ways of looking at the same manifestation, yet only Self Remembering will shed light on the third force behind your action, and three different people gave you this opportunity.

The key is in making an effort to not react when we receive an accurate photograph or observation that breaks through a buffer. The electric energy released at the moment, which can easily become a negative emotion, may be a short experience of our conscience. Truth itself is not an insult but time and again it offends false personality. As we are present during this experience, we see the features that stand for Pilate or Judas, trying to force us to look the other way. Yet at that precise moment we must make a further effort to not disappear and record the experience. Thus, if we use photographs correctly, we should be able not to buffer the next time the same manifestation comes to the surface. Every time the manifestation comes back, our steward must reappear in the form of an effort to separate from it. The longer we sustain the effort the stronger our steward becomes.

It is imperative that we focus on the message rather than on the way the message was delivered; and practice intentionally saying "thank you" right after a photograph, especially when the machine does not want to do it.

What proves that it is possible to apply this work "I" is that when we receive a photograph or an indication from the Teacher we are usually open and ready to work with it, at least initially. The same happens when we receive intentional photographs from students who are more awake in the moment. In other words, we have the device that can actually listen to what others have seen in us. When we access this device, the king of hearts, we are able to remember that our aim is to awaken our conscience. From there we can start making efforts to let the light in.

Higher Forces want us to create an Ark, but they keep us on an awful low budget.

Robert Burton

Donations

Every so often we experience negative I's about the donations we need to make in order to support our School. This tends to happen when there is a raise in the minimum donation, or the appearance of a special donation, or a new fund raising event. These I's may become strong in most students and not necessarily in those who have financial difficulties.

Needless to say that the part of the machine concerned with finances is the king of clubs; -remember we also call it: "the intelligence behind the machine". We can see the king of clubs as a boss, a father or a lord who is in charge of providing for its subjects, and he is constantly checking the way each and every part of the machine makes use of what it provides. It will therefore question the validity of anything we invest our money, time or energy in.

It wants to know things such as, who is that person our sex center is attracted to, what is the practical value of our friendships, how good is the job we are being offered. Of course it wants to know why does it have to pay a percentage of the money it earns, to an aim it does not directly and immediately profit from.

As many of us have verified, the last thing the king of clubs is interested in is the creation and maintenance of a School whose aim is to create consciousness in its participants. In fact, I do not know if there is anything it dislikes more than the energy of consciousness.

When we approach the question of supporting a real School on earth, we have to think in terms of transcending the machine. We have to think in terms of eternity, which is on a higher scale than that of the machine. Thus, we have to rely on higher parts in us, which can understand such potential. One way to evoke those parts is to make the effort to remember when we met the School and what urged us to join, and then explore the question.

It may well be that we joined the School for reasons other than awakening: well, this is a good moment to find out and act accordingly.

In any case, our School is designed for people who have seen they are asleep and who understand the necessity to work on themselves under certain conditions in order to awaken. Who is supposed to create and maintain such conditions? certainly not our mom, our dad, or the government. Think for example, who paid for the ticket of the student who moved to your city and opened a teaching house there?

The creation and maintenance of this School on earth, Apollo being its highest expression, is nobody's business but our own, yet because we all have a king of clubs, most of us have a hard time keeping the School and the Work alive. Regardless of how rich or poor we are, the king of clubs is always writing everything down and waiting for the right time to show us the bill. We know that. We know we are building our School and creating our Soul at its expense.

If you knew Time as well as I do, you would not speak of wasting it... It's him.

Lewis Carroll

How long have I been here...?

One of the dangers for us men number four is that false personality may lure us into thinking that the simple passage of time within the Fellowship of Friends, without effort on our side, will make of us not only older students, but wiser or more awake too.

The four lower centers are trapped in time; they know they have been in the School for a certain amount of years. Their memories are filled with experiences within the School and they expect to have got somewhere after all these years.

Although ours is a School of love, and it does accommodate circumstances not necessarily related to the Work, we know that simple association with the Fellowship does not guarantee that any of us is working on himself. In fact, many times we simply vegetate in complete oblivion of the reason why we came here, or fool around within the structure of the Fellowship. In general sooner than later lower centers learn to make themselves at home within the Fellowship. The instinctive center, for example finds within the structure of Apollo or its local center the most favorable circumstances according to its needs. It makes alliances with other instinctive centers. It creates its paths and places where it feels safe and taken care of. It creates its own curriculum within the structure and standards of the Fellowship. In short, it includes the School, the Teacher and Influence C in its own agenda. The emotional center in turn, either makes new acquaintances or brings its own to the Fellowship. It may even be grateful to live around people who try to behave in a noble way and to not express negativity. It appreciates being understood or cared for. The emotional center too has its own agenda, and so do the other three centers.

Sometimes, new students observe I's which imagine that students who have been longer in the Fellowship are for that sole reason wiser or more awake. On the other hand older students fall prey to these I's, and develop a patronizing or authoritarian false personality.

We must remember that a student is primarily someone who works on himself. The idea of an older student has to be applied in terms of experience in the Work, not in terms of time spent within the infrastructure of a conscious school. Even those of us who have played roles such as center director, traveling teacher etc, may have verified that these are not conscious roles, but rather roles of service that can be played more consciously, or less consciously. Sometimes we even run the risk of burying our conscience under such roles.

So when thinking about time spent in the Work, it is only fair to put together all of our study, all of the moments when we actually experiment, work on ourselves, make efforts not to express negativity, to stop imagination, control our feature. In short all of our moments of presence. That is the measure of the time we have spent in the Work. And what is more, that is our level of responsibility for the School and ourselves, regardless of when or how we joined the Fellowship.

In life, never do as others do.

Gurdjieff's Grandma

Feminine Dominance

Someone at a meeting described their main obstacle to awakening as their machine's tendency to seek approval from people, in other words, as the need to feel accepted and supported by the rest of their social herd. We approached this observation as an aspect of feminine dominance.

According to Girard Haven's definition we call this law feminine dominance in the sense that a child acquires it first from its mother during the process of learning acceptable behavior.

In the past we discovered that the king of clubs is the part of the machine that keeps us connected to the law of feminine dominance. The king of clubs creates an artificial device that will ensure the machine's psychological survival: false personality. Feminine dominance can thus be seen as a law that ensures the survival of humanity as a whole. The single individual is of no objective importance on the scale of organic life on earth, yet it has to feel important. Furthermore every single individual has to have the recognition of the rest of its social herd. This way its sense of importance remains intact. From this angle it is of no consequence whether the individual needs to feel respected or simply accepted by its social herd; whether it needs to feel superior, inferior, adequate, transgressive, aloof... it is all the same for organic life. What really matters on that scale is that every human machine is kept alive.

The machine is essence, its need to feel welcome and cared for is a legitimate birth right; every mother in nature provides this welcoming, caring environment. Essence is programmed to behave tolerably in order to ensure that this state of affairs continues. It will do everything it is expected from it in order to receive mom's attention and care.

In cases where the child is not properly taken care of, due to the inexperience or immaturity of the mother, its sense of worth is diminished; but it learns to attract attention anyway. Thus the individual's behavior tends to be transgressive or rebellious.

In a man number four, this condition sometimes makes him fall under the illusion that he is above and beyond feminine dominance, when in reality his behavior is simply the opposite side of the same coin.

Here are some observations in this regard offered by students during a meeting:

➢ Tendency to break the rules and exercises of the School as a way to work against feminine dominance.
➢ Tendency to question the Teacher and the form of

the School as the machine does with any sort of authority.
➢ Get always in trouble in order to attract help from other students.
➢ Mistrust especially of those who play a role of responsibility within the School.

The main characteristic of feminine dominance is the individual's need to be accepted within the social herd that ensures its survival. Whether one feels the best or the worst, great or insignificant, adequate or inadequate; one feels so in order to get recognition. This aspect of feminine dominance asserts itself in a different way in different machines. It is determined by the machine's center of gravity and chief feature. Here are some more examples provided by students:

➢ Need to be loved and accepted.
➢ Need to prove one is good at what one does.
➢ Need to feel the recognition of one's performance.
➢ Need to feel sexually attractive regardless of age.
➢ Demand for respect and need to feel feared by the rest of the herd.
➢ Desire to make allies with the strongest and most charismatic.
➢ Respect only those whom the king of clubs thinks are wiser or stronger.
➢ Imagination of being the center of attention.
➢ Expect compliments from everybody.
➢ Become a satellite of someone the machine considers strong.
➢ Fear of making mistakes.

➤ Make friends only with those who give reality to the machine's imaginary picture.

Again, we consider all of these observations from the point of view of the child in need to be accepted by its mother (social herd); primarily because it feels that she (it) is its psychological and biological survival.

"...If feminine dominance is indeed a way the king of clubs acts as a denying force to evolution, it would explain why the Teacher has given it so much emphasis." Girard Haven

This proposition helps us understand that to work on of feminine dominance implies work on the king of clubs. This in turn does not mean to hinder its legitimate pursuits, but to develop a different form of existence within the machine. To allow the king of clubs to do its job properly does not imply to neglect our own. In other words, our efforts to be present, to use common sense, or to be in good householder, do not necessarily mean to work against the king of clubs, in most cases they include its well being.

From this perspective it is not always necessary to change our external circumstances in order to work on feminine dominance, for indeed this is the true meaning of esoteric Work: it is invisible. The point is in doing the right thing for the right reason and at the right moment. In other words, while our actions may remain the same, the motive behind them will have a conscious origin, not a mechanical one.

Conscious acting replaces feminine dominance.

When we mature in the Work and start to be aware of the measure of our actions, we become more attentive to the third force behind them. We escape feminine dominance by changing our attitudes towards the very same events of our everyday lives. Of course we also know that some of our actions happen only when we sleep, as soon as we shed light on them, we cease to perform them.

Feminine dominance is necessary for children because they do not have real understanding.

When we manage to separate from the I's that seek approval from others we discover an odd paradox: most people are seeking our approval. Just as ours, their machines think they are at the center of the universe. This realization puts us in the position to make a further effort: namely withdraw the focus from our own machine and accept the fact that essence in people wants to feel loved, wanted, cared for and accepted. Here is where our possibilities of evolution stand, that is in trading our need of being taken care of and loved, for the understanding that people need to feel loved and cared for: we are then at the gates of external considering.

One way to work in this area is to try to make the same identical efforts as we often did before we started to work on ourselves, but with a different, more responsible attitude. Let's take some of the examples given by students in order to express this idea.

It is all right to be a good seamstress or a good mother, a good worker or a good husband, but with a clear understanding of what it means to perform that role with integrity. We can set the aim to perform our roles in life the best way possible, simply because we understand their highest possibilities, not because we expect the approval or the applause from people. Whether or not we get the applause or the approval from people does not depend on us, and it is in any case irrelevant to the task itself. Integrity is a capacity we can develop when we are in the king of hearts, and we can pursue it without necessarily disturbing the king of clubs; but we need to find the right concentration.

Let's now take the attitude that one should respect only those people the king of clubs thinks are wiser and stronger. If we consider that each one of us has a certain amount of wisdom and strength, we put ourselves in the position to learn from every circumstance and every person we happen to meet: we can then turn every situation to the best interest of our Work. But we have to keep in mind that in our present state, our idea of strength and wisdom is entirely subjective.

True wisdom has no preference.

With regards to the other side of the coin, that is the tendency to be transgressive or rebellious towards a given form of feminine dominance, a man number four can simply try to follow the rules with the understanding that he is trying to develop will, by exercising the practice of doing what the machine does not want to do.

The Teacher has said that feminine dominance is the law that keeps each planet in its own orbit. It seems that part of the work on feminine dominance is to try to consciously keep one's machine in its own orbit, which is something that already happens anyway. So it seems that in this area the machine does not have much to loose in any case.

Understanding avoids unnecessary and aimless friction.

Rodney Collin

What is Friction?

In "Fragments of an Unknown Teaching", Gurdjieff explains the condition of our psychological life with the following metaphor:

"Let us imagine a retort filled with various metallic powders. The powders are not in any way connected to each other, and every accidental change in the position of the retort changes the relative position of the powders... There is nothing permanent in the position of the powders and under such condition there can be nothing permanent."

First of all we have to verify, through Self Remembering and self-observation, that this retort, these different powders whose position is modified by accidental changes, are nothing but the machine and the many I's produced by mechanical influences. Unless we verify this state of things in our inner life, we will not understand the need to change anything. Gurdjieff goes on as follows:

"It is impossible to stabilize the interrelation of the powders in a state of mechanical mixture; but the powders may be fused, their nature makes this possible. ...The fire by means of which fusion is attained is

produced by friction, which is produced in man by the struggle between "yes" and "no".

In order to make this a practical thought we must ask ourselves what in us is *"yes"* and what is *"no"*. Before we understood the need to awaken, and therefore the need to develop an observing "I" or a deputy steward, the machine's tendency was to follow the line of least resistance. Thus the *"yes"* and the *"no"* in us were the mechanical forces that happened to converge in our field of awareness in the moment, and we simply followed the force that carried the most momentum or inertia.

When we start to make efforts to be present and observe ourselves, our relationship to the struggle between *"yes"* and *"no"* changes radically. On the one hand we have our aim to awaken, and on the other hand we have the great mechanical force that resists our efforts. In other words, friction, or the struggle between *"yes"* and *"no"*, begins with the aim to remember one's Self and observe oneself.

When we speak of friction we also refer to the stimulation of the negative halves of centers, which comes from the law of accident, the law of cause and effect and the law of fate. We share this forms of friction with most human beings and different forms of organic life on earth. The difference is that, unlike men number one, two and three, a man number four may profit from them. Every friction, small or big, when put in the right perspective, may be used for the development of will, for the creation of an observing I, for Self Remembering. Everything is useful, from a pain in the back to Income Tax, from our mother's death to the unpleasant manifestations of our boss, from the baby crying in the middle of the night to the School exercises the machine does not wish to put into practice. The Fourth way takes place in life, and though we sometimes do create small forms of friction to help us remain awake, mostly we have to make use of the friction produced by life itself.

Other ways of development create friction artificially. For example in the way of the fakir, the disciple has to remain in the same position for months or years on end. Some schools use fasting, or penitence, or seclusion.

We also receive friction from Higher Forces C, which is meant to help us work with our chief weakness or obstacle in the moment. We also have to learn to distinguish between friction given by Higher Forces from friction that comes as a result of our own ignorance, wrong attitudes or poor thinking. Given our almost hopeless condition, in the beginning it is not that important to try to figure out the origin of friction. For a long time we have to focus on developing the understanding that friction is a necessary factor for the creation of an astral body, so we can create the right attitude to use it.

As already stated, friction can be seen as the stimulation of the negative halves of centers. It would be a great step toward self-awareness to realize what center is activated by friction, or whether it is essence or false personality who experience friction. Next step is separation of our Self from whatever part in the machine experiences it.

When working with this tool, we have to detach from it emotions such as guilt. We also have to stop seeing friction in the Catholic way, that is, as punishment for sins committed in the past. Friction is a necessary factor for one who wishes to awaken; it increases the level of molecular energy within the machine, and we have to act upon this energy before it fades away. We have to keep in mind that divided attention is the way to control molecular energy.

The enlightened man guards his energy and does not expend it.

Hakuin

How we collect energy

Think of a formal Dinner at the Galleria with the Teacher. Before and throughout the dinner students help him in the effort to create a highly refined atmosphere. Cooking, serving and dishwashing are done intentionally. We dress formally; conversation is kept on a high level. Our behavior is collected. When Robert speaks, students pay special attention, thus his teaching falls on fertile soil. After dinner, the Galleria kitchen and salon are carefully cleaned and in the end they look impeccable. From one angle, dinners are a series of efforts to focus our attention with the aim to collect energy.

After a Dinner with Robert we are left with the energy of higher hydrogens, but oftentimes we do not know what to do with it. So the machine ends up eliminating it in various ways. Sometimes by hanging out in society and engaging in unnecessary talk or laughter, sometimes through rampant sex or infra sex, or unnecessary movements. Other times it simply feels "emotionally charged" during the following two or three days of the week, until the energy eventually fades away.

With some exceptions, students tend to be focused only when Robert is around, but once he is gone, we fall back to queens and jacks of centers, the main wasters of energy.

During the week we can create circumstances that will compel us to focus our attention with the aim to collect energy. We can, for example, organize formal dinners at our home. We may pick different students every time and make the aim to keep our energy before, during and after the dinner. We can also introduce voluntary suffering (friction, irritation, tension). This will pump energy from the basement to the upper floors in the machine. We may also initiate and finish ascending octaves (ascending octaves are sustained by effort). We may also try to refine our environment: clothes, kids, kitchen, bathroom (use Robert's home, the Galleria, as a standard): this will also produce energy.

Yet in order to collect and keep energy we have to be present as we receive it, and know the purpose of having it circulating within the machine, so that we do not get distracted and let it go. The energy we deal with is what we call "Higher Hydrogen"; the king of clubs will find it uncomfortable and will want to get rid of it.

Here is a tool we can use in this area. Every time we are exposed to a source of energy, (a dinner, a child, a painting or a color) make the effort to observe our state and then make a further effort to divide attention as we receive it. If the effort is right, we should be able to experience our essence as it is nourished with Higher Hydrogen: this is an aspect of Self Remembering. Try to work with one impression or event at a time for a short period, and then move on to another one until we get the feel of the effort, the feel of essence: the taste of our Self.

The final aim is to collect energy in order to create an astral body, one's Self. Every time one remembers one's Self, the energy one receives or produces is not wasted, but collected.

There are many tools designed by Robert or discovered by students that will help us make efforts, and thus produce more energy for the creation of an astral body. Yet we also have to make continuous efforts to stop leaks, for what is the point in creating more energy if our machine leaks all the time? It would be like filling a four-year-old kid's pockets with money knowing that he is going to let go of it at random.

Let us be happy, we are together but briefly.

Nahuatl Poetry

Nobility

Nobility can be approached as conscious acting in relation to people, humanity and life in general. It is a quality of our emotional intelligence, the king of hearts, and it can be experienced only when we are able to sustain that level of attention as we deal with these subjects. When we are in the king of hearts we acknowledge and respect every form of existence and its expression. So development of attention in the emotional center is the essential work in this area. In sleep, the instinctive center rules the machine's actions in relation to other people, even its closer ones. The reduced number of people the machine respects, loves, or feels compassion for, proves this.

Our king of hearts is nourished when we are exposed to the higher principles we find in philosophy, religion, art, esoteric ideas etc; but especially when we make the effort to apply them in our every day experience. Both the negative and the positive half of the king of hearts must work in unison in order to produce the right thoughts, attitudes, words, or actions towards people.

When we deal with people we must examine every action, thought and feeling in relation to them. We have to distinguish those which originate in the king of hearts from those which originate in other parts of the machine. This will increase our ability to be in the king of hearts.

Judgment, gossip, inner considering, negativity towards people, all represent wrong work of centers in relation to subjects where the king of hearts must be active.

Finally, we have to become aware of the third force behind our actions, for even though sometimes they seem "noble", we may discover that the third force behind them is some personal interest. In other words what looks like a noble action may be unconscious acting based on inner considering, fear, advantage, the wish to be acknowledged, or the need to reinforce the machine's imaginary picture of a good person.

Discovering the third force behind our actions requires the effort to divide attention, which is hard enough already. At this stage we do not know the third force behind other people's actions, we only have opinions about it, so it is better to acknowledge that we do not really know it.

It seems that the first steps towards nobility are self-observation and Self Remembering in relation to people: we cannot be careless when we deal with people. I believe both Christ and Socrates new what it took to bear the unpleasant manifestations of others. It partly meant to keep their own unpleasant manifestations for themselves, instead of expressing them towards others. In order to achieve that, they had to be very focused in order not to lose control of their lower functions.

Man is asleep; he must awaken in the right way.

Jami

Relativity

When Protagoras said, "Man is the measure of all things", he meant that truth is determined by every single individual's perception of it; in other words he saw truth as relative. Apparently he conceived men as unified beings, not as machines that produced many I's, depending on the function that prevailed in them in the moment. It seems that Protagoras did not know that even his thoughts originated in only one of his functions, which perceived things partially. He probably spent most of his life in the second state; and described only a way things look like when a man is in the second state.

If we spend our life in the second state, conscience is asleep, we believe every 'I' that happens to enter the field of our dull awareness. Thus we live under the illusion that we actually see the world and ourselves; and that we know the truth about these subjects. We may experience contradictory I's in relation to the same subject, yet every time any 'I' is expressed, when we sleep, we believe that it is the totality of our being and that we are right. Buffers prevent us from seeing contradictory "I's" at the same moment.

As we develop a deputy steward we verify that we are indeed in a machine that produces many I's. With practice, we also verify that they originate in the lower centers. However, our focus remains, not on the many I's, but on the creation of a deputy steward or observing 'I' and on the emergence of divine Presence within us. The deputy steward or observing 'I' is our ability to control our attention as we observe the I's. Here stand our possibilities to verify relativity in ourselves, for where else do we want to verify it?

Furthermore, only when we are able to control our attention can we aim to access the state of Presence. When we are present we see the I's for what they are and not as the totality of our being. That is, we know they are the result of the work of one center or feature. We understand they are momentary and, what is more important, our sense of identity is detached from them. This is, I believe, what Robert calls "to be in a state of relativity". We do not drown in the I's. We are aware of them and know where they come from. Even if we are not able to tackle them when they reach an interval, we may understand that they are unreal and short-lived.

Although sometimes we cannot engage Presence at will, we can still work from the deputy steward or the steward. That is, we can strive to control and focus our attention, study the machine through the language of the System, and observe the I's as we detach our identity from them.

Although it may start as theory, relativity is not an idea we can write down on a piece of paper and introduce in moments when we experience friction, but rather a quality of the state we are trying to pursue by constant effort.

Socrates used to say that the Divinity instructed him.

Xenophon

More on Influence C

I am sure every one of us has experienced more than once a connection with Higher Forces, yet we are not always able to remember clearly the price and the nature of that connection. One thing we know for sure is that we can only connect to Higher Forces when our higher centers are awake. Our problem is that we can hardly access higher centers at will and when we do so, it only lasts for a few moments at a time. On the other hand, most of us have verified that sometimes Higher Forces directly awaken our higher centers in order to establish a connection with us.

When higher centers fall asleep again, the memory of higher states and connection with Higher Forces remains recorded in lower centers. Thus, when we try to share them with other people (students or not), we do so in the second state, with people in the second state. We can verify this when we observe how some people react to our descriptions from their features. They either mock, scold, or put us down. Our chances of being understood depend both on our ability to articulate the message and the receiver's ability to control their I's and simply read or hear it without judgment.

Influence C do manifest in our lives, they address higher centers -most often higher emotional. The shocks they give us are meant to remind us of a definite fact: our conscience is trapped in the prison of our mechanics, and in order free it we need their help.

So we do receive shocks from Higher Forces meant to awaken us in the present, and do in the moment what conscience dictates us to do. Yet shocks are only the starting point for the effort to remember our Selves and act according to conscience. For some students, number 44^{13} is a shock that reminds them to be present and work, for some others, the name of a conscious being, for others a color, a word or the appearance of a humming bird. But as Ouspensky reminds us, external shocks do not guarantee that we will start making efforts from there. Our possibilities to awaken are in the effort to divide attention not only when we receive a shock or a sign, but always and everywhere.

Now, even if shocks come from Higher Forces, when we fall asleep they get assimilated into our dreams. Also, when we sleep, an ongoing sign-reading activity may ensue in the machine, which has nothing to do with our relationship with Higher Forces, it is only connected to the machine's organic existence.

---

13 When asked how many conscious beings are openly working with our School, Robert replied, "44". The number, a guideline of sorts, is used by students as a reminder to initiate the effort to awaken higher centers.

One of the hardest things in the world is to convey a meaning accordingly from one mind to another.

Lewis Carroll

Formatory Thinking

Formatory thinking is a Work term that describes the machine when it functions from its lower levels of attention, that is, the jacks of centers. Needless to say that in such case the observing "I", the steward or the deputy steward are not home.

When we are asleep and the machine is in the jacks, attention is obviously not controlled, the impressions we are exposed to do not reach us. Instead, the machine's memories and associations related to these impressions start to circulate in our intellectual center and are confronted with them. Thus, impressions remain at the threshold of our awareness. In our absence, the machine simply accepts, rejects, or labels what it sees or hears. Also, in our absence, this is what the machine calls "knowing". Apparently the sense of "knowing" is a necessary device for the preservation of the human species. Every machine has to have that certainty.

"Stick to words" said *Mephistopheles in Goethe's Faust, "they are the doors that lead to certainty".*

The king of clubs controls our most assiduous forms of formatory thinking, as the machine has strong preconceived ideas about subjects it is identified with. Some machines tend to be especially formatory in relation to sex and relationships, some in relation to ideas, some in relation to rules, yet others in relation to keeping the external form of a given organization.

In order to give up the machine's certainty we have to make it an aim to gain control of our intellectual center (just as for example, Socrates did) and little by little, one subject at a time, find our way to the full realization that we actually do not know anything about ourselves, other people, or the world. But first of all we have to remember ourselves in relation to this aim, for as Ouspensky hinted, we can only work when we are awake.

The king of diamonds is the best tool for the digestion of impressions for the intellectual center, but in order to use it successfully, we have to actually make the effort to control our attention. That implies to be able to think about one subject at a time, without deviating, considering it from as many points of view as possible, and to be able to tell what exactly we know about it, how much of what we know about it is heard of or read somewhere else etc. It also implies to take into consideration as many points of view as possible, from as many people as possible, for we know that our own machine's perception is limited. No machine is able to see objectively; machines only see what the device at work in the moment is able to see. In the second state there is an infinite number of ways of looking at things, none of them objective. This is probably one of the reasons why our Teacher keeps reminding us that for a long time, the only objective truth accessible for us is truth about ourselves: here is where psychological thinking comes into play, and it requires the kings of centers.

The priority of psychological thinking is the study of the machine as we separate from the I's it produces. Yet if we still wish to actually think about a different subject, Ouspensky's advice is very useful. As I recall he said, "Try to think about the subject itself, do no to think in opposites, you do not need to use such a clumsy method of thinking". In my experience real thinking takes time, it may take several hours... and it often leads to no conclusions.

If you ask what the word for the Presence is, we will reply the word "BE".

Ibn Arabi

Higher Centers

Sometimes we are able to see for a moment what it means to be in one particular machine and not in any other. For example from the moment he was created until the present moment. I see Rolando's inner contradictions, his limited repertoire of attitudes and features, his same old favorite negative emotions and subjects of imagination. This experience is connected to the work of higher emotional center. Perhaps the reason why it has "more of an emotional taste", as someone stated, is that the experience of higher emotional center is not about "man is a sleeping machine", nor about "the laws that govern the universe" but about "Rolando is a sleeping machine". In other words, it is about "I", the Self, trapped within this stimulus response machine (Rolando).

Rolando represents a certain type of prison, certain features and weaknesses that "I", the Self, have to experience, learn to recognize and separate from. Rolando is a role that produces a certain illusion, a certain way of interpreting reality. I have to study my way out of Rolando's limited perception of the world around him. In order to accomplish this, "I", the Self, have to awake and remain awake through constant effort.

Once we have acquired direct knowledge and developed the will to master the machine within which our conscience is trapped; once our higher emotional center responds to our will, then maybe we can pursue the effort to access higher intellectual center. The Self cannot ponder the nature of the universe unless it has fully emerged. Higher emotional center is within grasp; Self Remembering is the effort.

Although we can surely theorize and write pages and pages about higher intellectual, this experience is still not within grasp. It is a place we know exists, because we have experienced it, but we do not have the knowledge or the will to get there. In addition, our short experiences of this state will only be transmitted in a subjective way. Imagine for example, that while you are in the first state, you try to explain something to a person whose reality is determined solely by the nature of your dream. The person you imagine to talk to is not even there...

At present, we are still in the struggle to learn to distinguish and control the lower intellectual center, which keeps wandering and pondering the meaning of subjects that are none of its concern.

Whoever does not suspect his lower self at every moment has been fooled.

Abu Hafs

Mysterious Stranger

This letter was written in response to a question regarding Rodney Collin's suggestion to see oneself as an "interesting stranger".

None of us was there to really understand why Rodney Collin came to see himself as an "interesting stranger". Perhaps the insight came to him as a result of having realized his machine while in the third state, and he proposed it to his students as a Work "I".

Anyway, in order to use this as a Work "I"; that is, to see ourselves as interesting strangers, we must at least have the deputy steward active, for without this expression of our will, all we may experience is the machine thinking of itself as an interesting person. In general, every machine is bound to feel somehow special, different or interesting, which is a natural pacifier. I observe I's that feel interesting just because they happen to be Rolando.

The observing "I", the deputy steward, king of hearts, steward: all of that stands for our ability to control our attention and direct it towards the study of the machine as we try to separate from its functions; or, as someone suggested, the role wherein our Self has been cast this time. Therefore we are in the position to see our machines as interesting strangers, or simply as machines we are interested in studying, when we are controlling and dividing our attention. Other times we see them as simple devices, which serve a purpose on a scale so great, that it does not consider them as individuals.

We may wish to question, what is interesting about Rolando, Ellen, or Tina? Would it be as interesting to be Frank, Douglas, or Girard? To successfully apply this work "I" requires a certain quality of attention, and the relentless effort to separate our identity from that which we observe. Our true identity is sustained by the effort to separate from the machine, whether or not we find it interesting.

The sole fact that Rodney Collin suggested this as a Work 'I' does not necessarily make it a useful "I" for us. But we certainly turn it to our favor when we are able to see where it does originate: Self-Remembering is necessary.

No effort? No Self-Remembering.

Act in such a way that the opportunity may not pass you.

Mahabharata

Opportunity Lost

We have to take into consideration the scale and level of what the machine calls "a lost opportunity", as opposite to what we, as men number four, consider "an opportunity". On the level of the machine, we miss planes and buses, soccer games, job opportunities, chances to apologize, etc. On the level of the machine the I's worried about a missed opportunity come from the emotional and the instinctive center; and are connected exclusively to the machine's subjective idea of what should have or should not have happened. In the beginning, working with the I's identified with having missed an opportunity may be an intense experience, because the memory is still fresh in the queens and this makes identification strong.

Depending on the level of development of our steward and the level of identification of the machine's imaginary picture, working with this type of identification may take a few minutes, a few hours, a few weeks, a few months. But we have to focus on the fact that working with it makes our steward stronger. We will eventually to be able to work not only with future similar identifications, but with other types of identifications as well. Of course if we do not work with them, we run the risk of carrying the load of our undigested experiences for the rest of our lives. On the other hand, with time even our strongest sweet or sour experiences vanish. So we have to transform the hydrogen they produce before time takes it away from us.

Because we are men number four, every time the memory of a lost opportunity on this level comes back, that itself is an opportunity to separate from lower parts of the machine: queens and jacks. This is a different level of opportunity, for it is connected to awakening.

As men number four we see opportunities from the point of view of Self Remembering, self-observation, the effort to change our level of being etc. Thus opportunities present themselves every moment of our lives, if we loose one, another one comes right the next moment: so we do not need to waste time thinking about having lost one. At times it is the opportunity not to express negativity, the next moment it is the opportunity to separate from the I's that identify with failure for not having being able to do it. Or to separate from the I's that feel proud of themselves because we were able to do it. Sometimes we are trying to be present to an impression, then next moment we move on to not judging or mocking people... thus the Work is an inexhaustible source of opportunities:
Carpe Diem!

It's all her fancy, that: they never execute nobody, you know.

Lewis Carroll

The Queen of Hearts

The machine has a device designed to weight and question the legitimacy of people's behavior. This device, the emotional part of the emotional center, is constantly scanning and sorting peoples' behavior in relation to the machine and its social environment (just like the queen of clubs does with food, the weather, other instinctive centers, etc).

When confronted with people, the queen of hearts instantly checks in detail body language, gestures, tone of voice, manners, intensity of the eyes etc, in order to know where people stand in relation to the machine's essence, or imaginary picture, and its social environment. Thus it quickly reacts in terms of good and bad behavior -its understanding of good and bad is based on its own demands. Every machine has a queen of hearts, but some of us are centered in that card.

I work with this mechanical center of gravity: probably the instinctive part. This means I have verified that the machine focuses on people and their behavior, more so than on impressions or ideals. When it gets interested in impressions (landscape, art, music) it does not go into so much detail as it does with people.

The queen of hearts is a fairly accurate organ of perception of people, but it is only the perception of external behavior, it cannot perceive the third force behind their actions.

It also spends a lot of time producing i's about people after having interacted with them. Yet it does not produce noble or ideal I's, as the king of hearts would, but rather it focuses on their reliability or inconsistency in their behavior. Later it goes on to make up theories about the reasons why people are this or that way, and it also likes to communicate these theories and perceptions to its friends.

The instinctive element (5 of hearts) is seen in the fact that the queen of hearts perceives people almost exclusively in relation to the machine itself, or to its social environment: School, family, country. It almost never questions the machine's own behavior (in fact, it is fascinated with its own behavior; it enjoys being the way it is). The king of hearts instead, will weigh behavior (including its own) in terms of a greater whole: humanity, a society, a community. The queen of hearts is a level of attention not suitable for thinking about people or transmitting impressions. In order to think or act emotionally in relation to people, it is necessary to raise my attention to the level of the king of hearts.

As already said, the queen of hearts is very sensitive to what people do in relation to the machine, but paradoxically it is insensitive to its impact on people. Thus it tends to photograph tactlessly in the moment.

Photographing is a Work tool it makes free use of. Photographs from the negative half of the queen of hearts in areas of identification are delivered with a sense of urgency and a desire to evoke shame in the other person.

In fact one can loose friendships due to the activity of this card. But being its center of gravity, the machine does not care too much about it, for it feels safe and relaxed only with those people who do not represent an emotional threat.

The queen of hearts expects perfection in human behavior. I discovered this when I used to work as a photographer at teaching events. The mechanical tendency was to take pictures of students only when they were at their best. This required that I spent a lot of time simply watching students through the zoom, and refrain from shooting unless the moment was perfect. That is, when students displayed their finest emotions.

Sometimes the queen of hearts works together with other cards:

Queen of diamonds: It goes through different phases of interest in people it considers remarkable. One time it gets interested in Tarkovsky, and then Queen Elizabeth I, Joan of Arc, Cristina Rossetti, Robert Burton, Bach, Purcell, Socrates, Giordano Bruno, Lincoln, etc. It is not interested in literature for its own sake, or in cinema or music in general, but rather in the man or woman and what they achieved in their particular area of work.

Queen of clubs: Reads in the moment body language, gesture, tone of voice, intensity of the eyes, clothing, age, use of words and general attitude in people as it interacts with them. When left to its own devices, it interprets or makes up a story of its perceptions.

I would also like to add that one can only observe and study all of this impartially when one successfully hides it from others: it is an intense experience. More intense than to let it express itself in its own sweet way.

Before the creation of the observing "I" the imaginary picture of the machine was that of a passionate sensitive man, yet from the third state, the queen of hearts is indeed perceived as a prison.

The queen can be seen as a symbol of power, the king as a symbol of will.

Thy actions to thy words accord.

John Milton

To Be the Words

* While some ideas will remain theoretical or philosophical for us, there are others that are always within grasp, but we have not verified them or have not tried them due to oblivion or lack of will. "To be the words" is a Work term we use when we begin to become aware of the gap between our knowledge and the use we make of it. Because part of our Work is to keep the System ideas circulating within the School we end up knowing and talking a lot more than we can actually do. For a long time we are bound to keep repeating and rewriting the same concepts over and over, sometimes without understanding their meaning. Thus, "to be the words" sooner or later has to become a pursuit for us. But in order to be the words, we first need to determine exactly "what words" we want to be.

We may start from a Work idea or a theory. For example: the development of a steward. Then get all the information regarding that idea: try to read about it, ask questions about it. What is really a steward? Is it a level of awareness? Is it attention sustained? How do we perceive the machine when we are in that level of attention? In short, we need to make sure we know what steward means; and don't forget it.

Then set an aim connected to it. For example the aim

could be: "To observe the activity of the instinctive center without judgment, without trying to change anything; just observe, record and make the effort to detach our identity from what we observe". That would be a function of the steward; that is, being able to control our attention and try to separate from what we observe. One cannot understand the meaning of steward unless one makes continuous efforts "**to be**" the steward. Conversely, one cannot "**be**" the steward unless one "**knows**" what in theory a steward is.

Thus a link between "**to know**" and "**to be**" is to have an aim and to make efforts connected to what we know: a clear, short aim and constant efforts. It is essential that we share our aims with other men number four, so that we are often reminded to pursue them, for as stated before, we tend to forget ourselves.

There are many subjects of the Work we may explore from the point of view of being the words, and all of them revolve around the effort to remember one's Self, because if we want to be the words we first need to **be**.

Freud spent his whole life in the second state, trying to study the first state.

Robert Burton

Work Language

This was written in response to a question regarding the reason why we have to use the language of the System in order to communicate with each other. The student asking the question also shared an observation regarding the tendency in the machine to use what it calls "emotional language", language from other systems, such as Astrology, and in some cases the language of ordinary psychology.

As far as I understand, an esoteric work language is created by or through men who have their higher centers active, and it is designed to help those who are asleep connect to higher centers. The form and nature of this language vary, depending on the nature of the people it is intended for and their cultural context. Work terminology is comprised of precise instructions. One of the first instructions we are given is to set aside terminology and concepts from other sources if we wish to learn it successfully. The language of our System is designed for men number four, but not by men number four. From the point of view of the System, emotional language, for example, is the language of man number two produced in sleep: it may sometimes sound poetic, yet it is subjective, since it is meant to communicate one way a given machine decodes reality.

We are not expected to modify or improve the language of the System, we simply have to learn it and put it into practice. Thus, one of our aims in the School is the study and verification of the ideas of the System through self-observation and Self Remembering. As we learn to master the System terminology, terminology from other sources is seen as a deviation or, at best, as coincidence.

Older Systems and work languages are B influence, that is, the conscious source which produced them is no longer available. In my experience, false personality uses them for self-gratification or as pacifiers. Amongst others we may mention the *Bible,* the *Mahabarata,* Dante's *Divine Comedy,* the various Astrology manuals, the Tarot etc. Regardless of how fascinating they might seem, they are like dead languages; what gave them birth and kept them alive has ceased to exist. It would take a conscious being to regenerate them and decode them for us.

Some of these languages were part of our magnetic center, and they may even have inspired our first line efforts for a while. Yet sharing our experiences in the Work with other students is second line of Work, and we were given a precise Work language for that purpose. Additionally, we have to take into consideration that other students may not be acquainted with the "foreign language terminology" we try to introduce in our conversations, so we cannot expect them to fully understand us. I personally have no knowledge of Astrology, yet in the beginning, when I was not able to express myself in terms of the System, I made use of other languages, like Carlos Castaneda's or my first Teacher's. Later on I realized other men number four in the School understood me better when I used Work language.

As for ordinary psychology, one of the reasons we call it so is that ordinary men, or sleeping machines, have created it with the aim to guarantee balance in the second state. It is not meant to awaken higher centers. Again, if we still choose to use it we run into the same difficulty, other students may not know anything about it.

Like in any learning process, it is difficult to be in the kings of centers and express ourselves in Work language, but it is always possible, and so simple that false personality thinks it is flat or boring. If at one point there is something we cannot put in terms of the Work language, we may ask for other students' help, as there are many who know the System very well, not only in theory but in practice too. Leading or attending prospective student meetings helps us understand unclear observations: the aim is to attend these meetings with a learning attitude.

Sometimes the real difficulty is that there is no apparent difficulty, since there is a seemingly innocent "I" that thinks some things seem impossible to translate in terms of the System ideas, thus creating a buffer that prevents us from making efforts. We know false personality likes to complicate things in order to avoid real work. Therefore it is essential to figure out what part of the machine is this "I" coming from and detach our identity from it. Put this "I" in terms of the System: i.e. is it coming from the steward?

In a mind that loves rightly, the love of God is valued more than the love of man.

Bernard of Clairvaux

Identification or Love

When we are identified, most likely we deal with others through the king of clubs, the queen of hearts, the jack of hearts, the sex center etc. A way to find out what part of the machine is interacting with other people is to try to determine the third force behind our thoughts or actions in relation to them. When we sleep, the king of clubs might monitor even the most innocent or caring of our actions. A way to verify this is to observe the machine when it is negative with its close ones, and see the basis of its accounts with them. We might be surprised to find out that a lot of our good deeds are based on some kind of personal gain or fear to lose the favor of our close ones.

When we deal, think or talk about people, besides the effort to divide attention, we must make the effort control our attention in the emotional center. A sign that we are acting from the king of hearts is when we divide our attention and see ourselves studying others from the point of view of their needs, their likes and dislikes, their hopes and fears; or, if they are students, from the point of view of how we can help them in the area they are working with in the moment (if we have been asked to do so). This implies that our own needs, likes etc, have to be put in perspective and considered from the point of view of how they aid or hinder the well being or the work of other people. When we are in the king of hearts we are able to keep in mind what others expect from us, both in relation to their needs and to our mechanical behavior. And we are ready to sacrifice our subjective ideas of what is best for them and for their evolution.

Identification with others: (partner, offspring, strangers, work mates, friends), is also called inner considering. Inner considering has two faces, one is the feeling that we owe something to someone else, the other one that someone else owes something to us: respect, recognition, admiration, care, or help. Inner considering originates in the king of clubs and is kept alive by the queen of hearts. The king of clubs does things for people because it wants to ensure its emotional and instinctive status in relation to them.

When we act from the king of hearts we are able to respect and care for all forms of life. The difference between our close ones and other people is that we know more about them. Thus we are in a better position to offer the right form of external consideration in the moment; be it a photograph, a hug, a snack, or simply leaving them alone. A way to prevent identification in this case is to create the attitude and eventually come to the full understanding that we do it because we have verified that this is the best we can do for them. Our own moods, opinions and chief feature have to be kept under control.

In the Fourth Way, respect for sex and a positive attitude towards it are fundamentally necessary.

R. Collin

Sexual Attraction

This article is based on a letter written in response to a question about the legitimacy of attraction towards the machine's same sex, and the feeling of inadequacy or uniqueness that springs from such mechanical tendency.

The nature of the sex center is independent from the machine's programming in relation to sex. Also, it is a fact that some machines experience sexual attraction towards members of the same sex. It is as mechanical as the fact that most machines experience attraction towards members of the opposite sex. The same law is manifesting when we see how a piece of metal is attracted to a magnet, it does not stop to think what shape, color or semblance the magnet has: the metal simply is mechanically attracted.

Attraction is based on chemistry. One may observe attraction towards some people, but not towards all people, there are some "types" towards which one's sex center does not react. They might be good-looking in terms of the model of beauty proposed by a particular society, but the sex center simply does not get activated.

However, although one may experience attraction towards some types, the king of clubs may not be interested if they have reached a certain age, or seem unripe... In this area the king of clubs sees no men or women, but males or females: males as potential competitors, females as potential bearers of its seed. If the female vessel is too old, it will not bear good kids, if it is immature, it will not be able to raise them properly.

Another observation is that sometimes the machine gets interested in people displaying various kinds of behavior, regardless of type. For example, the queen of clubs may be drawn towards women dressed especially to attract male's attention: mini-skirts, black stockings and similar items of clothing. On the other hand the emotional center might be attracted towards women who show a certain amount of suffering in their body language and attitude. In this case, it is not sexual attraction but interest on the level of the queens. In the first case the stimulus implies the promise of the enjoyment of the sensual aspect of sex, while in the second case the stimulus evokes the desire to soothe the person's pain.

When one follows a line of action based on such stimuli, one may attract a relationship not exactly based on sexual attraction but on instinctive or emotional interests and/or tendencies. There are also other reasons unrelated to sexual attraction that may cause one to get interested in entering a relationship; in fact they are related to personality. For example sometimes the instinctive center gets interested in someone else's social or legal status. Other times the emotional center is in search of a paternal or maternal figure, or it is simply trying to get out of a situation through a relationship.

Being married does not alter the machine's tendency to feel attracted towards other men or women. Of course when one is committed to one's partner, or to a higher aim that requires the use of the same creative energy, one has to constantly keep mechanical attractions in check: it is a question of economy. In that case one has to transform sex energy related to attraction into presence, and prevent the instinctive center from acting on it. On the other hand, although at the beginning of a relationship there is usually a strong attraction between partners; in time it might cease to be as intense. This only means that a relationship has to grow beyond its first mechanical impulse.

"Sexual desire is not the only form of love. It is tremendously important, and may carry deep spiritual love on its tide. But when it diminishes, the other forms of love must not be thrown away with it." Rodney Collin

Consider the analogy of the magnet and the metal, or two magnets bearing a similar force of attraction. The closer they get, the stronger the energy that draws them together, yet once they have finally come together, the force inevitably disappears. They cease to be two objects attracted to each other and become a unit, a single whole; and this unit, this single whole, must have a purpose.

We have verified that the sex center has no negative parts, it either recognizes an attraction or it does not. When it experiences attraction there is the sense of legitimacy, and the machine does not have a mechanical device to stop it. In order to control the activity of the sex center, one has to develop a different device for it, an artificial negative part, so to speak. For a long time we do not have to worry about finding this artificial negative half, since every society has one way or another of feminine dominance to keep human sexual behavior within reasonable limits, according to its own standards. On the other hand one's own feminine dominance in this area is a good subject of study.

We know the king of clubs is the brain that keeps us connected to feminine dominance. And that its main aim is to make sure the machine reproduces itself. The most primitive aspect of this is the male thoughtlessly trying to spread its seed in as many young female vessels as possible. In the case of the female it would be to choose for fecundation the fittest, strongest and most able male vessels, and discard them once their duty is done.

In a patriarchal society, the male king of clubs controls the female. A man in a patriarchal society has to make sure his woman or women bear his seed and not someone else's. For example in Italy there is a saying:

"May you give birth to male kids". Male kids ensure the survival of the family's name (the herd). While female kids are a potential threat to the herd, they may burden it with unexpected kids from a different breed for example, and in the best of cases they will eventually leave the herd and join a male from a different one.

When a male born within the herd is not able to perform, either because he is impotent or because he is attracted to other males, the king of clubs within the whole of the herd rejects him, thinks there is something wrong with him. This is probably why most societies give a hard time to machines with homosexual tendencies, since they do not fulfill the main purpose of their existence. In other words, they do not guarantee eternity for the king of clubs; the same applies to female machines attracted to other females.

These are the rules of the instinctive center, and the instinctive center rules the mass of humanity.

Yet different principles rule our lives. Our sex center (whatever its tastes and inclinations) is for a long time a subject of study and work and not a point of reference for the search of an identity. Anyone interested in self-study and self-development will have to learn to be present to this center and observe the way its energy is borrowed by other centers and vice versa.

Another observation in this area is that there are times during the year in which sex energy is not really directed towards mating or having a relationship. The machine is simply not interested in it at that time. Sex in relation to mating responds to specific cycles, and it is different for different races and machines. However, there are a couple of issues that make this aspect of our study complex. One is the fact that, especially in the western world, man has isolated himself from the climatic influences that determine procreation cycles; we live in an air-conditioned environment. Another issue is that, while animals mate solely when the female is suitable for fecundation, western man has developed a habit to remind himself of physical sex (through fashion cinema, advertisement, etc) in virtually every aspect of his existence. With this in view, it might take one several years of neutral self-observation in order to understand one's own machine's particular cycles.

It is useful to observe that when one finds oneself thinking or pursuing sex for its own sake outside of these cycles, one might be procrastinating in other areas of one's life, such as householder, friendship, work on first, second and third line, plus one is feeding the very force that keeps one asleep.

The sex center is the fastest of the lower centers; it is even faster than the observing "I". The observing "I" is a function of the intellectual part of the emotional center. So the only way to observe the activity of the sex center is to remember one's Self while it is active. Otherwise one has to study it through the trace it leaves... which might prove to be a vague way of studying the machine.

A good source of information (and work) in this area is one's own partner. Partners are inevitably aware of each other's sex center activity, simply because their king of clubs is especially concerned about not being taken advantage of or abandoned. In some cases partners can provide each other with precious information in terms of the use and waste of sex energy. In order to exchange information in this area, though, one has to control one's attention at the level of the king of hearts and try to think in terms of "the machine and its lower functions" and not "me" or "I" or "you". Negative emotions such as fear, jealousy or mistrust are not welcome into this study; they just make it clumsy and sometimes are quite destructive.

Waste of sex energy happens not only in relation to mating, "falling in love", or compulsory physical sex. Sex energy leaks into all four centers, through negative emotions, unnecessary talk, and imagination. Observation of this type of wrong work will keep one busy for a while. One observation in relation to imagination, for example, is that a certain amount of creative energy goes into the making of the scenes the machine wishes to imagine.

Sometimes we feel the hydrogen of sex circulating within the machine in the moment, either because it is springtime or because there is a clear stimulus in the environment. A certain substance is released within the organism, which spreads faster than any thought or emotion. Nothing is more pleasant, nothing more soothing, nothing more fascinating for lower centers. It does not matter whether the stimulus is a man or woman, in these cases we need to have the aim to just let go of the stimulus and use the energy to be present. When we succeed in this practice, and we focus our own presence: that is Self Remembering.

There is no limit to the practice of Self Remembering, that is, it is also right to remember one's Self in relation to sexual attractions. The advantage in these situations is that the energy necessary for the creation of the astral body is already circulating within the machine. When the effort to remember one's Self does not accompany the experience of sexual attraction, the very substance one's soul is made of literally flies away. The fact that Self Remembering is the highest use of sex energy helps us understand that we can always transform the activity of the sex center.

In relation to the part of the question about the uniqueness of being homosexual, it really makes no difference whether one is homosexual or heterosexual but vanity finds every reason to feel unique since one way or the other it does not matter, we are all alike, facing the same difficult choices.

Finally, Self Remembering does not interfere with the way our hormones work; nor does the way our hormones work interfere with Self Remembering. On the other hand, if homosexuality is not the result of the work of one's hormones, or if one believes one is sexually attracted to a person simply because they emit sex energy, Self Remembering will shed light on those fallacies too...

http://livingpresence.com/

www.ingramcontent.com/pod-product-compliance
Lightning Source LLC
Chambersburg PA
CBHW021822090426
42811CB00032B/1976/J